Differentiated Instruction in Art

Art Education in Practice Series Marilyn G. Stewart Editor

Artmaking, Play, and Meaning Making
Assessment in Art Education
Community Art in Action
Engaging Visual Culture
Race and Art Education
Rethinking Curriculum in Art
Roots of Art Education Practice
Talking about Student Art
Teaching Meaning in Art Making
Therapeutic Approaches in Art Education
Thinking through Aesthetics
Using the Art Museum

Heather L. R. Fountain

Differentiated Instruction in Art

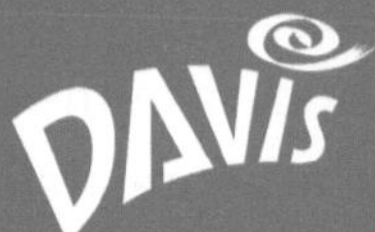

Davis Publications, Inc. Worcester, Massachusetts
DavisArt.com

Series Preface

Follow an art teacher around for a day—and then stand amazed. At any given moment, the art teacher has a ready knowledge of materials available for making and responding to art; lesson plans with objectives for student learning; resources for extending art learning to other subjects; and the capabilities, interests, and needs of the students in the artroom. Often shifting several times a day from working with preschoolers to those in elementary, middle, and high school, the art teacher decides what to teach, how to teach it, whether students have learned it, and what to do next. The need for rapid decision making in the artroom is relentless.

The art teacher's day continues after school with student learning assessments, curriculum planning, organization of materials, and activities within the school community. Although most teachers want to stay current with new findings and developments in their field, finding time regularly to keep up with the literature is a challenge. Art Education in Practice provides the art teacher, museum educator, student, scholar, and layperson with an overview of significant topics in art education theory and practice. The series is designed to meet the needs of art educators who want to think critically about the issues, rationales, and practical implications of accepting curricular proposals, with input from a variety of scholarly and political perspectives.

The series emphasizes informed practice. Each book focuses on a timely, relevant topic from art education literature and advocacy statements, and connects the ideas to the classroom. The goal of the series is to complement the professional libraries of practitioners in the field of art education and, in turn, enhance the art-related lives of their students.

Editor's Introduction

Art educators often find themselves in conversations about *what* they teach. In casual encounters with colleagues, for example, we might share stories about lessons we've taught, artists we've introduced to our students, art materials we've discovered, and studio projects incorporated into our programs. In more formal contexts, administrators want to make sure that what we teach—our course content—is consistent with national, state and/or district standards. There's talk about teaching the 21st Century Skills, along with discussions about the how art educators will address content specified as the "Common Core." Within the pervasive culture of assessment, we also find ourselves engaged in conversations in which we attempt to articulate the art content that is most important, which means, of course, important enough to be targeted for evaluation.

With all of this focus on content, I am reminded of the oft-repeated slogan, "We teach *children*, not subjects." When taken literally, the slogan is false, since children must be taught *something*. However, like most educational slogans, this one has significant practical import. It reminds us that in deciding what we should teach, we need to remember those whom we hope will gain from learning the selected content. We need to consider *whom* we teach, along with the *what*. Additionally, as part of the process of focusing on our students, as we come to understand who they are as individuals, how they learn, and what they need, we may well be prompted to rethink the importance of certain identified content.

The author of this text, Dr. Heather L. R. Fountain, takes very seriously what it means to know our students and to remember that their individual ways of being in the world must guide the daily pedagogical decisions we make. Most teachers recognize that students learn best in different ways, and many dedicated teachers have long sought ways to address these differences. For art teachers, especially, the process of noting individual interests and abilities often becomes an intuitive part of teaching. It's what we *do* as art teachers.

It's one thing to recognize differences among students, however, and yet quite another thing to know how these differences might be addressed in a dynamic and productive classroom setting. Dr. Fountain draws upon her many years of K–12 and university teaching, as well as her extensive research in the area of differentiated instruction, to assist her readers in their attempts to create such classrooms. She provides solid theoretical perspectives and highly practical strategies for teachers wishing to pay careful attention to *whom* they teach, along with considerations of *what* they teach. In the end, this is a book about excellence in teaching.

Readers are in for a treat. I have had the honor of working with Heather Fountain at Kutztown University of Pennsylvania, where we are colleagues on the faculty. This book project derives from her deep devotion to her students, and to her goal that each and every one of them experiences success in her classes. Modeling for her students as well as her colleagues, Dr. Fountain lives the life of teaching that she proposes throughout this exceptionally informative and useful text. I feel confident that it will be transformed into a well-worn and marked-up handbook as dedicated readers refer to it over and over again throughout their own experiences in teaching.

Marilyn G. Stewart

Acknowledgments

This work is to honor all teachers who dedicate their time, money, and lives to providing the best opportunities and experiences they can for all of their students, each and every day. For such as these, happiness is found in doing what they love, because they know it is an honor and a joy to teach.

I would like to extend my deepest gratitude to one of the best teachers I have ever known, my father. He was a true warm demander who cared deeply for his students, yet held them to high standards. His example taught me what Differentiated Instruction was, even before I knew it myself.

For me, Differentiated Instruction first came alive through the dedication and hard work of the individuals I worked with at Mary Rowlandson. I thank you for working as a team to turn an imagined school, one where all children are considered gifted and their ideas count, into a reality. It was that reality that fueled my passion for teaching and armed me with the tools I needed to help all students, regardless of their background, reach their highest levels of success. In addition, I would also like to thank my colleagues and students at Kutztown University for their support, ideas and passion for art education.

Finally, I would like to thank the team at Davis Publications for their dedication to publishing quality, accessible art education texts.

Heather L. R. Fountain

Publisher: Wyatt Wade
Series Editor: Marilyn Stewart
Senior Editor: Jane McKeag
Design: Tyler Kemp-Benedict and Douglass Scott
Copyeditor: Deborah Thompson
Proofreader: Victoria Hughes Waters
Editorial Assistant: Missy Hall Nicholson

Library of Congress Catalog Card Number: 2012952530
ISBN: 978-1-61528-121-3 paperback
978-1-61528-122-0 digital

10 9 8 7 6 5 4 3 2 1
Printed in the United States of America

Contents

Download reproducible resources and worksheets at DavisArt.com/DI/Resources

Introduction

"A mind that is stretched by a new idea can never go back to its original dimensions."

Oliver Wendell Holmes

As a teacher, the most significant moments in my life have been those when I have seen students arrive at that amazing "Aha!" moment as their eyes light up with understanding. You can almost see the cartoon lightbulb appear above their heads while the look of excitement spreads across their faces. They have finally made the connection and are as proud of themselves as you, their teacher, are of them. Whether the student is age three or ninety-three, it is just as rewarding to have helped someone reach that place of understanding. For some students it happens immediately or easily, but for others it takes great amounts of effort, sometimes even tears, to arrive at that gratifying moment of comprehension.

In my continual search to increase these moments of perception, I started to read about ways to develop powerful learning in my classroom. I found descriptions of learning that were interactive, real, exciting, connected to students in personal ways, and spiral in nature. This concept of learning laid a foundation of knowledge and then built upon it with new knowledge that spiraled students to higher levels of understanding. Part of this concept included a belief that you must understand your students and where they are coming from in order to design lessons that could help them—all of them—reach greater success in their education.

This is the search that led me to an approach called *Differentiated Instruction,* which helped me discover a whole new level of teaching that almost immediately benefited my students, my school, and me. It changed good teaching into great teaching by helping me learn ways to get to know my students and use that information to build strong lessons that connected with them and got them excited about learning and about art.

Differentiated Instruction, often called DI, also helped me create an artroom where all individuals are part of a community of learners; where each is valued as a unique and important part of the whole. It transformed the classroom into a safe place where students know that they have individual and unique strengths and ways of learning, and where they respect each other's differences as artists and as learners. My students not only learn about art, but also about themselves and each other.

One of the greatest struggles I encountered in trying to implement Differentiated Instruction practices into my teaching was due to the lack of art-related examples of DI and the disconnect between how the information applies to the art classroom when compared to general education classrooms. The books and articles I found were all directed toward teachers in the general education classroom who often see the same students every day. Like many art teachers, I did not have the luxury of a consistent schedule with twenty to thirty students I saw on a daily basis. I taught hundreds of children.

My schedule consisted of six to seven classes each day of students of various grades whom I saw for forty-five minutes once in every six-day schedule cycle. This schedule averaged a meeting with each class approximately thirty times throughout the course of the school year, and this average does not take into account the occasional missed class due to Monday holidays, snow days, fire drills, field trips, or assemblies. I was constantly asking myself, "How am I going to modify or translate this information to make it work for me?"

At this point, like most art teachers, I had become fairly adept at doing just that—translating what I was reading about general education and making the information applicable to the art classroom.

This book is meant specifically for art teachers to guide them in the use of Differentiated Instruction in their classrooms. It is based on the experience I have gained by implementing its methods into practice within my own classrooms, as well as by consulting in schools, teaching Differentiated Instruction to other art educators, and conducting research in classrooms where teachers were already using DI.

Since 1999, I have been teaching others how to use Differentiated Instruction to enhance their classroom practices. For every moment that I have helped others strengthen their pedagogy, my own has been empowered as well. Their ideas and lessons are as much a part of this book as are my own and I thank them for their ideas and contributions. It is my hope that this information will guide you, the reader, in connecting with Differentiated Instruction and will inspire you to find ways to light up the eyes of your students with a love of learning in and through the arts. My wish is that Differentiated Instruction will be as much of an "Aha!" moment for you as it was for me.

The chapters in this book will take you on a journey through Differentiated Instruction; each chapter is broken down into content that addresses the most common questions that I receive about DI. Chapter 1 answers the question, *What is Differentiated Instruction?* In successive chapters, you will gain deeper insights into the information provided in this introductory chapter.

Chapter 2, "History and Foundations," will explore the theoretical foundations of Differentiated Instruction by answering the question, *Where did Differentiated Instruction come from?* This chapter will help break down many of the theories, ideas, and best practices in education that comprise and shape Differentiated Instruction. With this basic knowledge in hand, chapter 3, "Why Teach This Way?" will help you consider why you might choose to implement DI in your classroom and what the benefits for you and your students could be. This chapter also includes the personal perspectives of teachers and students who have experienced Differentiated Instruction in their classrooms to help you make connections and answer this question for yourself.

In chapter 4, "One Teacher, Many Roles," you will begin to think about the personal question, *How will DI shape my role as a teacher?* You will explore the concepts that describe what it means to be a Warm Demander, a Partner in Learning, a Proactive Designer, a Flexible Manager, and a Reflective Practitioner.

Differentiated Instruction can function differently in various settings or classrooms and you can implement it in multiple ways; for this reason chapter 5, "Getting Started," will help you consider the question, *How would I start to implement DI in my classroom?* You will learn small, proactive steps that you can take to design curriculum and instruction that help to maximize students' ability to connect to learning. You will also consider what role pre-assessment plays in assisting you and your students to accomplish their learning goals.

Chapter 6, "Curriculum," and chapter 7, "Differentiated Lesson Examples," help you explore in greater detail numerous practical ways to implement Differentiated Instruction in your curriculum, while providing examples that help to contextualize each strategy. The examples provided span all grade levels and, for each lesson, break down what you will differentiate and how.

Chapter 8, "Tips for Success," the closing chapter, will share experiences of how to find and build support for yourself as you begin your journey into Differentiated Instruction. It will also provide tips on how to deal with those who don't understand what you are doing, as well as how to advocate for your choice to teach in this way. Following this chapter, you will find an appendix of additional resources.

Chapter 1

What Is Differentiated Instruction?

"The biggest mistake of the past centuries in teaching has been to treat all children as if they were variants of the same individual, and thus to feel justified in teaching them the same subjects in the same ways."

Howard Gardner

"I can't do this; I'm just not good at art!" How many times have we all heard this in our classrooms? I am sure that you, like me, have some tried and true responses that you pull out of your art teacher's tool kit when you hear this exclamation. Two that I often used were "YET! You're not good yet, but you will be!" and, "Not everyone likes or is great at all types of art. Maybe painting is not your thing, but I bet you will find something you are really good at as we work with other media and ideas."

My statements acknowledged that I knew my students had different strengths and weaknesses, levels of readiness, and likes and dislikes; we all do. We are all different and engage in the world differently. I myself am a hands-on visual learner. If I am to understand something, I need to see it and touch it. This is very different from my husband who needs to read extensively about something before he picks it up or interacts with it; he is the one who reads the entire manual that comes with new products. We interact with the world around us very differently. One method is not more appropriate than another; it's just different in the way it accommodates our needs and learning styles. This reality is the same with our students' learning styles.

As teachers, we have become increasingly aware of the broadening spectrum of abilities that students use to learn and acquire knowledge, and as a result, we are searching for ways to respond to students' diverse needs. Differentiated Instruction, a term coined by teacher Carol Ann Tomlinson, uses a multifaceted approach to help teachers discover ways to meet the needs of *all* learners in the same classroom. Differentiated Instruction is not just a way of thinking about teaching and learning. It encompasses a collection of best

PERSONAL CONNECTIONS

Taking Stock

As you read, consider the following questions:

1. What is your ideal learning environment? What would it look like? Feel like? Sound like?
2. Think of your favorite teacher. What made her or him your favorite? If you didn't have a favorite teacher, what qualities would your favorite teacher have had?
3. In what ways did your educational experience help you thrive or prevent you from thriving as a learner?

practices and strategies that help teachers respond to the wide array of student needs present within their classrooms. At the very heart of DI is a teacher's desire to maximize the potential of all their students by guiding them to achieve higher levels of learning success. Achieving such a goal is not always easy, but we can accomplish it through the proactive use of differentiation to design both spaces and learning experiences that provide all students of diverse learning styles the choices to access knowledge in different ways.

An Overview

Differentiated Instruction involves the interaction of three key interdependent elements: teachers, students, and curriculum and instruction. These three elements help provide teachers with direction when designing curriculum and instruction to meet the needs of their students. When these three elements are in harmony, teachers are providing the appropriate balance of support and challenge to draw students into meaningful learning that engages them and keeps them connected.

Teachers provide:

- **Opportunities** for students to be involved in learning through important real and attainable ways.
- **Unwavering support** that helps students believe in themselves and reach higher levels of accomplishment.
- **Investment** in students that shows them that they matter and that they are worth their teachers' time.
- **Reflective practices** that consistently assess teachers' actions and their students' actions, needs, hopes, and fears as a way to guide future classroom practice.

MAJOR POINTS

Teachers Are a Bridge to Understanding

Not all students learn in the same way or need the same things to feel secure in taking the risks that learning asks of them. The teacher who provides a bridge of understanding and safety in the classroom enables students to connect to learning.

- **Acceptance** that respects students for who they are and invites each of them to be an important partner in learning.

Students receive:

- **Challenge** at appropriate levels that stretches them and helps them believe in their abilities.
- **Interconnectedness** in learning so they know that they are an important part of something outside of themselves.
- **Independence** to make decisions and know that they have power in and control of their learning.
- **Affirmation** to know that they are accepted, that they matter, and that someone believes in them.
- **Connection** so that they understand how and why their accomplishments are important and significant.

Instruction:

- **Helps students make connections** to their lives and their world by building on prior knowledge or experiences.
- **Engages students** so that they are excited about learning.
- **Offers attainable yet demanding goals** so that students experience both the support and the educational opportunities that allow them to experience challenge and success.
- **Values trial and error** as a way to grow and learn.
- **Has purpose** that does not simply fill time but uses it wisely to help students gain essential knowledge, understanding, and skills.

The Foundation of Differentiated Instruction

Differentiated Instruction is not a prescribed set of specific steps to follow in a certain order to create an ideal classroom, but rather it is an approach to teaching that is informed by a combination of best practices and beliefs.

The following set of beliefs forms the foundation of Differentiated Instruction:

- Students voices and perspectives are valuable.
- Teachers should empower students to think critically and make decisions about their learning.
- Students learn differently and have different learning needs.
- Students start their learning at different points.
- To teach students effectively, when designing curriculum teachers need to be proactive as they consider students' learning differences.
- Even though students may be reaching for a similar goal, instruction may not look the same for all students, or the same at all times.
- Ongoing assessment is the key to designing a strong curriculum.

Considered individually, these core ideas are not unique to DI, but when combined, they create a powerful philosophical framework on which to build.

To put Differentiated Instruction into practice is to recognize students' varying background knowledge, skills, interests, current experiences, readiness, personal cultural development, learning styles, learning rates, learning challenges, language

MAJOR POINTS

Student-Centered Learning

Differentiated Instruction is a student-centered approach to teaching. Students are valued and the consideration of their voices, ideas, backgrounds, and needs is integral to classroom instruction.

proficiency, motivations, ability to attend, physical needs, and social and emotional development, and then to use this information to help students learn in a safe atmosphere where their differences are valued.

We already know that our students vary in many ways, but it is often overwhelming to consider how we might use this information. DI provides us with a way to address these differences and use them to engage students in activities that better respond to their various learning needs.

THINK POINT

Reaching All Students

A friend called me to ask for advice at the end of a long school day during her first year of teaching. After a troubling incident with a student, another teacher had advised her that the student was beyond reaching and not "worth her time." Are there students who are not worth our time?

How do you view students?

Predetermined

- Intelligence is fixed; how smart or talented someone is cannot change.
- Genetics and environment determine who students will become.
- There are some students whom teachers will never reach.
- There are some students who can't learn.
- Some students are not worth my time.

Growing

- Intelligence is fluid; students are always learning, growing, and changing.
- Genetics and environment help shape who students are, but with persistence and hard work most students can shape their own future.
- All students are worthy of having great teachers who continually challenge them.
- If students don't learn the way I teach, then I need to teach the way they learn.

We can gather this information, the key to reaching and teaching all students successfully within the classroom, through straightforward pre-assessment tools and observation or through more formative assessment methods. The art teacher can design and implement a strategy of assessment using such tools, when needed, throughout the school year. With this pre-assessment information, we can proactively design differentiated lessons in ways that connect individually to all students.

Retaining Individuality vs. Individual Instruction

MAJOR POINTS

Responsive Instruction

Differentiated Instruction is not Individualized Instruction but, rather, responsive instruction. Teachers do not create separate lessons for each student in their classroom. When designing a lesson, a teacher responds to learners' needs by creating one lesson about a particular topic that has one, or a combination of, the following items:

- Varied modes of delivery, experiences, or interactions.
- Varied methods for students to demonstrate newly acquired knowledge.

Differentiated Instruction is often confused with Individualized Instruction, popular in the 1960s, which recognized students' different learning needs by attempting to create different lessons for each and every student in the classroom. This method of instruction was extremely time-consuming because it required a teacher to create twenty to thirty-five different lessons, one for each student in his or her classroom. Most often, students worked individually and on different topics. Although Differentiated Instruction and Individualized Instruction have a common goal of meeting the individual needs of each learner within the classroom, they have different configurations and means of implementation.

With Differentiated Instruction, students most often work on the same topic, but sometimes in different ways. The objectives of the lesson are the same for all students, but the way they reach them might be different. Teachers can accomplish this by providing a variety of means to access and learn about the same content. Differentiated Instruction helps teachers create learning options in a classroom that assist students' ability to access knowledge in different ways. These options could be related to how the topic is taught, learned, or demonstrated.

THINK POINT

Is Equal Fair?

Fair is being equal and treating all my students alike, right?

Consider the process of learning as providing your students with ladders that will help them reach their learning goal. In an equal classroom, the teacher would provide the same ladder or instruction to all students, ensuring that they all have exactly the same resources, which seems fair.

In this case, having the same length of ladder did not help students who were in different places to reach the same goal at the same time. Some students were able to reach the goal, while others never had a chance because they were not starting in the same place as others. In *Fair Isn't Always Equal,* Rick Wormeli defines Differentiated Instruction as doing what is fair for students by providing them with the tools they need to "maximize students' learning at every turn."[1]

Differentiated Instruction is a collection of best practices, strategies, high expectations, support, and appropriate challenges that ensures all students have an equal chance to learn and grow. Being fair is giving all students what they need to succeed; sometimes that means using different types of ladders to reach the same goal.

Students don't start off at the same place in learning; they have different backgrounds, experiences, and levels of knowledge. Providing the same ladder or method of learning to all students is not fair or equal, as some will never have a chance to reach their learning goals.

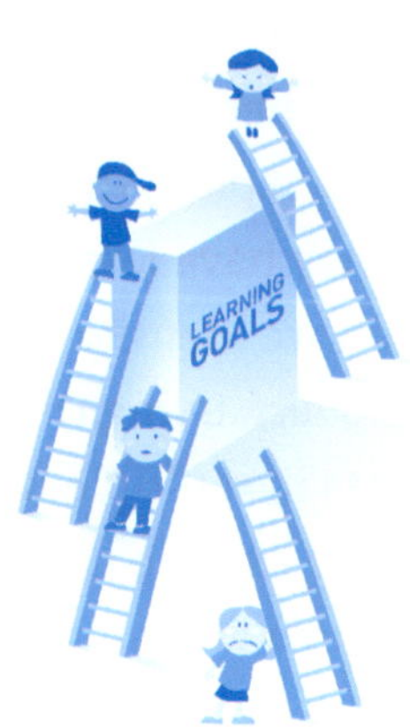

Differentiation provides different ladders or methods for acquiring knowledge that help all students have opportunities to reach their learning goals.

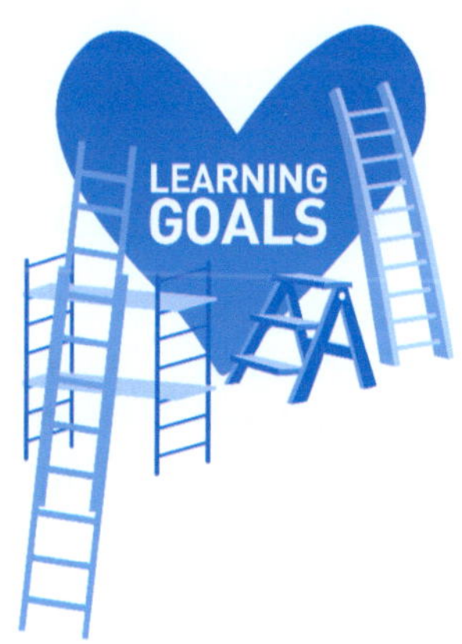

An example of creating a differentiated lesson would be for a teacher to create one lesson idea that includes three different means (visual, auditory, and kinesthetic) for learners to engage in learning. A teacher might also differentiate lessons in response to students' needs by changing the pace, level, or type of instruction that their lessons provide.

DI is more than simply giving students choices or offering different options to students; it is distinguished by the teacher *designing* instruction that takes into consideration students and their learning needs and styles. Although student choice can be a powerful way to engage students, choice alone does not ensure that students meet their learning goals, unless the choices are specifically designed with that in mind.

Implementing Differentiated Instruction in Lesson Planning

MAJOR POINTS

Curriculum Differentiation

We can differentiate three areas of curriculum:

- The content—the objectives students will learn.
- The process—the method by which students will explore and discover the content.
- The product—what students will do to demonstrate what they have learned.

A significant element of Differentiated Instruction is the consideration of how teachers design instruction. As teachers, each time we create a lesson, knowingly or not, we consider at least three lesson components: the topic we are teaching, how we will help students explore this topic, and how students will demonstrate what they have learned about the topic. In Differentiated Instruction we identify these three components as *content*, *process*, and *product*. Using DI, we can differentiate each of these components in multiple ways for various reasons. In the next section, we will explore each of these components and look at examples of how we can differentiate them.

Content

Content is the "what" of Differentiated Instruction. It is what teachers want their students to learn and be able to do. Think of content as the topics, themes, and concepts that you will

MAJOR POINTS

Assessment

Assessment is an important part of Differentiated Instruction.

Pre-assessment helps teachers know:

- What prior knowledge or background experiences students have as they enter into a learning environment.
- What students' interests, learning styles, multiple intelligences (see p. 37) strengths, and challenges might be.

Formative assessment helps teachers know:

- How students are progressing during a lesson.
- What areas of instruction the teacher might need to clarify.

Summative assessment helps teachers know:

- What students know and are able to accomplish as a result of their learning.

teach your students. Your school, school district, and state government often determine the classroom content using written standards. However, teachers can differentiate content when they focus students' attention on key skills, processes, or concepts by varying the complexity of the learning at hand. Teachers can achieve this focus in one of the following ways: pre-assessment, subtopic exploration, or readiness matching.

Pre-assessing students' skills and knowledge about a topic will allow you to use that information to match learners, according to their readiness, with appropriate activities. This became very helpful for me with one particular lesson related to weaving. I assumed that my students had little knowledge about weaving because I had not covered that topic before, so I decided to pre-assess them on the topic. I found that they already knew the basics, so I was able to skip my planned lesson and create two options that helped students learn about weaving in greater depth without wasting our precious class time relearning skills and knowledge that they already knew.

This allowed me to make a deal with my students: If they could show me that they knew some basic, level one concepts such as warp and weft, and could create a small weaving, they could pass on to level two. This type of differentiation is a very effective way to reduce student boredom and apathy, while ensuring that all are challenged to grow and stretch in new directions. With pre-assessment, if some or all of your students can demonstrate knowledge of and competency in a topic, then they need a more challenging option to help them continue to grow in this content area.

Another way to differentiate content is to give students choices about subtopics they can explore in greater depth. This is very effective when students need to learn about a topic that they can explore collectively or in a more general way. In many schools, including the schools where I have taught, there are often curricular topics such as Japan or ancient Egypt that are required content at certain grade levels. These topics are often very broad and students can explore them in numerous ways. This type of topic is a perfect candidate for content differentiation in which students can learn about various aspects of the larger topic.

Content differentiation also provides students with the opportunities to become experts in a specific, chosen area of a larger topic. This type of content differentiation also allows you to choose topics and resources of varying complexity, ranging from sophisticated and technical to basic, and to match them to a student's prior level of understanding of that topic. For example, if you know that a student in your class is more of an expert on cartooning than other students, he or she may be given a different and more complex subtopic such as political cartoons to investigate. This allows you to challenge your advanced students and keep them interested in learning. You can find an example of a summarized lesson that uses this type of content differentiation at the end of this chapter and in Fig. 1.1.

The third way teachers can differentiate content is by providing students with basic and advanced resources that match their current levels of understanding about a topic. Currently, many art teachers are asked to incorporate more reading and writing into their curriculum. This can be challenging when you have students with a wide range of readiness for reading and writing represented in your classroom. In this situation, a teacher could differentiate content in terms of readiness by providing three readings about a similar topic that have varying levels of complexity. This would ensure that all students could

LESSON EXAMPLE

Differentiating through Content

In the lesson *Ancient Egyptians: Who were they?* the expectations were the same for all students in the class. Students were expected to:

1 Explore ancient Egypt through four areas: leadership, life, culture, and art and architecture.

2 Build communication skills.

3 Work cooperatively within a group or team.

4 Utilize various resources to conduct research.

5 Demonstrate acquired knowledge.

Students chose two areas of focus, selected by the teacher from the school district's curriculum guide, (leadership, life, culture, and art and architecture). The teacher used these choices to group students into investigative teams. This structure allowed all students to have investment in their topic because they chose it, while ensuring that students were distributed evenly within the groups. The teacher gave each team a folder that included Internet, book, image, and artifact resources to explore.

After two classes, the teacher placed new instruction sheets in the team folders. These instructions guided the teams to decide what they needed to research further over the next class period. The teacher also included a section on the instruction sheet that provided choices on how to interactively teach their newly acquired knowledge to their peers.

In this example, the content is differentiated in a way that allows different students to work on different content subtopics under a unifying larger topic. All students learned about all four sub-topic areas, but each team had invested heavily as experts in one area. The teacher in this scenario was a guide or mentor, ensuring that all teams were on-task and had covered the content they were charged to explore and teach to their peers.

Ancient Egypt

1 Students selected an area of focus:
- *Leadership* – government, religion
- *Culture* – food, music, dress, burial
- *Life* – social status, education, jobs, roles
- *Art & Architecture* – homes, monuments, palaces

2 Each group conducted research and discovered information about their topic through artwork, artifacts, and online resources.

3 As experts, each group interactively taught their peers about the topic they had researched.

1.1 Differentiation by Content: Ancient Egypt Design by Heather L. R. Fountain and Karen Primiano.

successfully engage in reading about the chosen topic, but they could do so at levels that make learning attainable and appropriately challenging.

Process

The differentiation of process is involved with the "how" of instruction. When a teacher focuses on the process of a lesson, he or she considers how students will engage in learning about the content. This involves the teacher deciding how to organize the classroom instruction and the strategies or interactions employed to aid students in engaging with the learning goals, as well as other considerations such as whether students will work individually or collaboratively in groups.

A teacher also needs to consider his or her students' readiness and abilities when designing how they will engage in the process of acquiring knowledge. These considerations can lead to a significant variation in the type of instruction and can involve any strategy or action that helps students think through the topics they are learning. It could be as simple as reading and reflecting or as complex as experimenting with materials, collaborating with others, or evaluating artwork.

When learning through differentiated processes, simple variations in media choices, grouping of students, or types of interactions can be quite effective. In addition, adding or removing elements of complexity in a lesson can call on students to use and apply critical thinking skills that match their levels of readiness. It is important to note that through the differentiation of process, all learners are engaging in the same content knowledge while taking advantage of opportunities to consider that knowledge in different ways.

LESSON EXAMPLE

Differentiating through Process

There are numerous ways for individuals to consider or make sense of what they are learning; therefore, there are many ways in which to differentiate the process of learning that can take place in a lesson. In the following example, the process is differentiated through variations in the art media used by students as a way to help all students access art learning in ways that meet their developmental and physical needs.

After reading aloud a story about a flame of peace to my first-grade class,[2] the students shared their examples and definitions of *peace*. Using collage techniques, they individually created their own images of a monument that represented peace. I differentiated the process of creation through the use of three stations where students could work in various ways that helped them find success in art-making even though they had varied levels of physical and developmental functioning. Two options for each station were set up in the room for a total of six separate stations.

- **Station one** involved the use of various papers; three kinds of scissors—traditional, left-handed, and adaptive scissors; and glue sticks.
- **Station two** had assorted papers, paintbrushes, and watered-down glue in cups. Instead of using scissors, students would have to use their hands to rip, tear, and shape the paper.

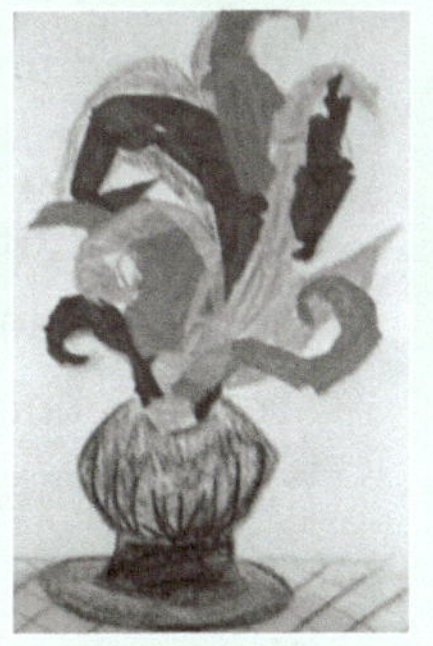

1.2. *Flame of Peace.* A student's representation of a peace memorial that uses crayon, various colors of ripped tissue paper, and cloth.
Photo: Heather L. R. Fountain.

- **Station three** included various papers, white glue in squeeze bottles, and three-dimensional found objects such as buttons, twigs, leaves, sand, and cloth.

On the first day, I assigned each student to work at one of the three stations according to their various physical needs and learning styles. On the second day, I gave students the option to stay at their original station or to visit the other stations as they worked to finish their projects.

This assigned method of grouping ensured that every student could access learning successfully and be appropriately challenged according to their specific needs, yet it provided enough flexibility for them to explore other methods if desired. Students with tactile sensitivity and differing levels of motor skills worked in ways that helped them to be successful while challenging them to grow.

MAJOR POINTS

To Differentiate or Not To Differentiate

It is important to understand that most learning experiences can be differentiated in some way, but that it is not necessary or possible for everything to be differentiated all the time.

Product

Product is what students have done or created to demonstrate what they have learned about a topic; it reflects what students know and are able to do as a result of their learning. This is often the easiest area of the curriculum to differentiate, because it involves student preferences and choices without a lot of initial teacher planning. Often, when a teacher gives students choices, they will select the option that naturally matches their learning strengths and preferences.

The product can be as varied as the students. Models, brochures, reports, speeches, debates, skits, art-history research, mock trials, dance, visual art production, podcasts, and videos are only a few of the options that students could use to demonstrate their newly acquired knowledge. Through differentiation of product, a teacher may choose to offer two or three options or to allow students to make proposals.

Teachers also may design the product to be specific and undifferentiated in one area and nonspecific and differentiated in another. For example, all students may be required to research and write a report about an artist they are studying, but could have a differentiated option that allows them to represent visually one of the big ideas used in the artist's work through varied choices such as a painting, sculpture, or video.

LESSON EXAMPLE

Differentiating through Product

Differentiating a lesson is often as simple as building product options around students' interests. In the following example of a lesson about clay techniques, the objectives were the same for all students and met the requirements set forth by the school district, but the teacher built some element of choice into the assignment. All students participating in the lesson explored the use of clay tools, building techniques, texture, and safety, but they had choices about how they would individually demonstrate their newly acquired skills.

In his high school Art I course, Nick Urffer struggled with ways to help his students find value and interest in art. One of his major goals was to help students find something they enjoyed in education, with the hope they would stay in school. With this in mind, he decided to modify his lesson on clay techniques to incorporate three choices related to his students' interests.

To create product choices that would best connect with his students, he pre-assessed their interests by asking them to write one thing they liked about the class on the classroom whiteboard before they left for the day. He used this feedback to design two choices, and added an open-ended choice as a catch-all for students who wanted the freedom to explore an alternate idea. As illustrated in Fig. 1.3, after making their choices, students worked on their clay sculptures using their personal interests to explore and meet the objectives of the clay lesson.

Using Personal Connections to Create Choice

Objectives:

- Students will apply the concept of texture within their projects.
- Students will research one or more concepts to assist in making informed decisions about their work.
- Students will create a 3-D clay work that includes the use of two or more methods of building. (slip, score, coil, slab, etc.)
- Students will use clay appropriately with safety and care.

Choose one:

A. Research and choose a word that has a relationship to texture, and strengthen its meaning by designing a visual representation that shows what the word means.

B. Research, design, and complete a real or imagined animal of your choice. Decide what textures this creature should have to make it look realistic.

C. Create a proposal of something you would like to research and create using clay. Present your idea for approval.

1.3 Product Differentiation Example: Personal Connections Created by Nick Urffer and Heather L. R. Fountain.

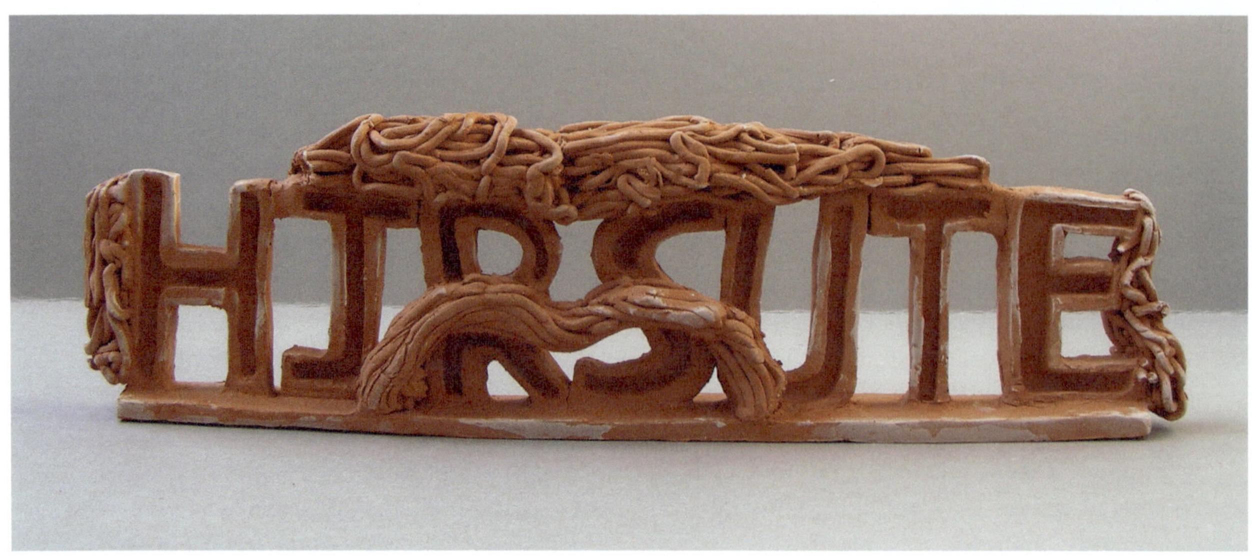

1.4 *Hirsute:* A student's favorite word became the inspiration for his clay sculpture. Do you know what hirsute means?
Photo by Nick Urffer.

The design of this lesson engaged all students in the same content and process of learning, but differentiated how students demonstrated the knowledge and skills they had gained through their product choices. Differentiated product choices allow all students to follow their individual interests, cultivating ownership of the choices they have made, and they are therefore more invested in the creation of their artwork.

Another unique and positive aspect of product differentiation is that it usually leads to greater variety in the completed student works. In the example above, students became very engaged in creating and researching the topics they had chosen. The studio tables were covered in books, printouts, photos, magazines, and Internet resources that students had brought into class to assist them in designing their product. The choices that students made varied greatly and ranged from a favorite word—*hirsute* (see Fig. 1.4)—to a platypus (see Fig. 1.5) and even to Bigfoot.

Other students focused on the textures they wanted to make and created slabs of highly textured surfaces to use in creating their word-art pieces (see Fig. 1.6).

In this class, students were focused and connected to their products through their interests. One young man even stated that he couldn't wait to bring his sculpture home to place on the shelf in his room.

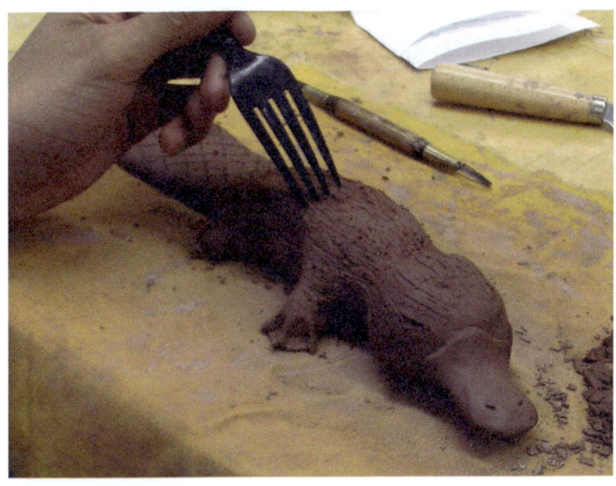

1.5 *Platypus*. A student works to add texture to a favorite animal. Photo by Nick Urffer.

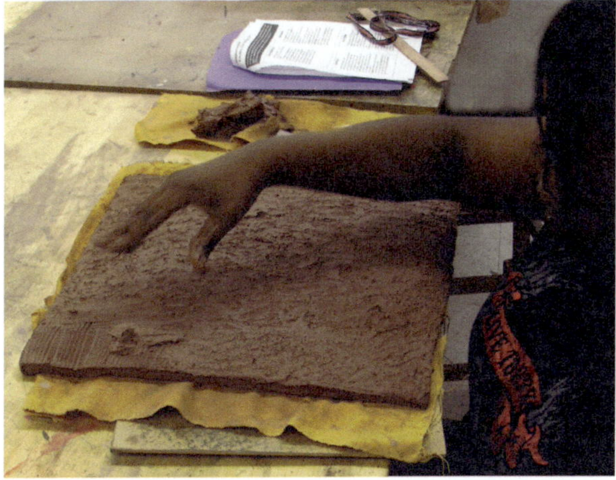

1.6 *Textured slab*. Students used various tools on a slab to create textures that they associated with their chosen words. Next, they cut out the letters needed to illustrate their sculptural word (see Fig. 1.7). Photo by Nick Urffer.

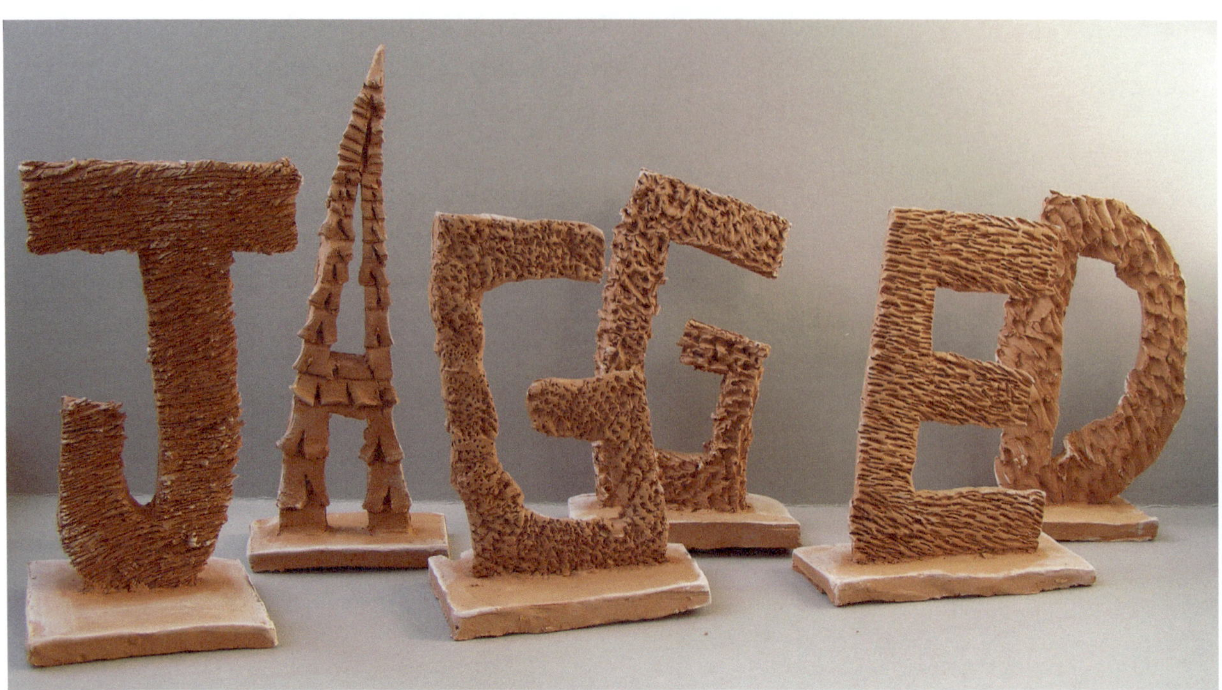

1.7 *Jagged:* Both the word and the texture are jagged. Photo by Nick Urffer.

Conclusion

By giving teachers tools to purposefully refine the structure of lessons that reveal to students the varied means to access knowledge in and through art, Differentiated Instruction can transform a classroom into a community of active, engaged learners. This structure not only recognizes students' differences, but also values those differences and validates each student's ability to make choices about his or her own learning. This consideration is precisely why learning looks different in a DI classroom—not all students learn the same way, nor do they have the need to learn the same things at the same time due to varied levels of prior knowledge.

The following chapters will help to further describe DI and provide tools and examples to aid in the understanding of how DI can look, in action, within the art classroom.

REFLECTION & PRACTICE

Taking Stock

1 **Valuing Students** In what ways do you currently help your students thrive as learners by valuing their perspectives and their different ways of learning? This week, think of at least one way that you can clearly show your students that you value them no matter who they are. Think of one student each day this week that could most use your encouragement and find a way to connect with them.

2 **Beliefs** In this chapter, you read about the beliefs that form the foundation of Differentiated Instruction. Revisit that list and circle the beliefs that match your own philosophy, even if you have not fully figured out how to implement the beliefs. Next write down other beliefs that are important to you about student learning. If you are not sure where to start, consider writing the following prompts on a page and use them to help begin your reflection: I believe that students deserve... Strong teaching looks like...

3 **Connections** After reading the first chapter, consider what aspects of DI already exist in your classroom or teaching philosophy. In what ways do you already offer choice in the products students create? Think of one or two ways you can intentionally differentiate the content, process, or product of a current lesson this week so that students have varied ways to interact with the lesson.

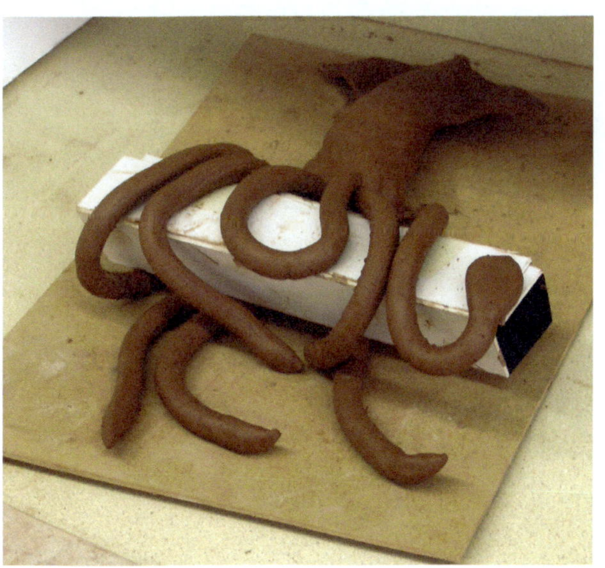

1.8 *Giant Squid:* After extensive research, a student created a giant squid with tentacles specifically propped in a way that would allow her to insert something into its grip once it had been fired. Photo by Nick Urffer.

Notes

1 R. Wormeli, *Fair Isn't Always Equal: Assessing and Grading in the Differentiated Classroom* (Portland, ME: Stenhouse Publishing, 2006).

2 D. N. Lattimore, *The Flame of Peace: A Tale of the Aztecs* (New York: HarperCollins, 1991).

Chapter 2

History and Foundations

"The road to success is always under construction"

Arnold Palmer

MAJOR POINTS

Where Did Differentiated Instruction Come From?

Differentiated Instruction is not a new trend or concept, but a combination of many educational best practices that have been shown to help students make significant gains in learning.

PERSONAL CONNECTIONS

Understanding Learners

As you read, consider the following questions:

1 How do you currently make art learning relevant to your students?

2 What type of learner are you? How does this affect your teaching style or classroom?

3 What structure do you use, if any, to organize your curriculum in a way that makes sense for learners?

When I first began to learn about Differentiated Instruction, I thought it was something completely new that my school was trying to institute. I soon realized that the ideas behind DI had existed for quite some time and many of them were educational practices with which I was familiar or had already used. I discovered that what was new about DI was the intention to combine well-established educational practices and use them with purpose toward the goal of helping all students learn and grow to their best abilities. Differentiated Instruction was not some trend or fad, but rather a new term that defined a combination of extensively researched and proven practices that, when used purposefully, could have amazing results for my students and my school.

Theoretical Foundations

The term *Differentiated Instruction* was coined by educator Carol Ann Tomlinson in the early 1990s. As a classroom teacher, she sought ways to help all students become engaged in learning. After a continual process of reflective practice (which she would say is still ongoing), she began to write about her classroom instruction so that others could share in the same success she had in helping students connect with learning. This type of instruction combined best practices in education with well-respected theories and research from the fields of education, psychology, physiology, brain research, and motivational research. It is important to note that DI is not one educational method or philosophy, but a combination that helps teachers and students create powerful learning experiences.

Differentiation is a synthesis of what research has taught us (best practices) about how students learn best and how best to teach them.

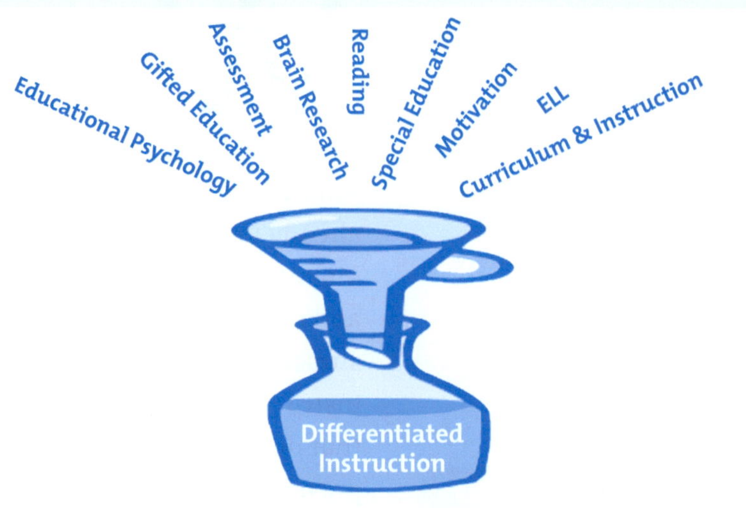

2.1 *Best Practices* Designed by Heather L. R. Fountain and Carrie Miller.

Knowledge about teaching and learning has continued to expand as research and classroom practice reveal insights about the brain and its ability to access, process, and store information. This knowledge persists to help us as teachers and action researchers discover new practices and strategies that augment student learning.

The elements that form the foundation of DI are all practices that have been known individually to aid teachers in understanding and teaching students in amazing ways. They are the work of prominent educators and researchers over the past century; you may already know many of their names or their work.

Constructivist Theory

The constructivist values found in DI draw their foundational ideas from educator and researcher John Dewey. In the early half of the 1900s, Dewey asserted that education often failed due to its inability to connect with students and involve them in learning. He objected to an education system that had as its mission the delivery of information to children as if they were empty vessels waiting to be filled. As stated by Dewey and embodied by Differentiated Instruction, an effective curriculum takes into account students' differing needs and actively involves them in the process of making decisions about their education. One of the greatest changes in the American education system was Dewey's call for students to become active participants in learning instead of students sitting in rows, listening to lectures, or reciting memorized information.[1]

Based on Dewey's educational philosophy, many progressive schools were created and teachers began to design experiences for their students to discover, explore, and create knowledge in interactive ways. This approach also changed the teacher's role from what many have referred to as a "sage on a stage" to a partner, or mentor, in the learning process, guiding students to discover independently meaning within a subject. By incorporating these considerations into a curriculum, all students are assured the opportunity to participate in quality educative experiences that help them discover knowledge and make connections.

Many current educator-researchers such as Grant Wiggins and Jay McTighe, who wrote *Understanding by Design*,[2] and Stewart and Walker in their *Rethinking Curriculum in Art*,[3] also advocate the use of constructivist theories in education, so that teachers develop classroom environments in which learning is *relevant* to students.

Brain-based Theories

What we do know about the brain through modern neuro-science has enabled us to understand how students learn and, therefore, how we can best help them plug in to learning.

MAJOR POINTS

Helping Students to Learn

It is essential to find the right amount of challenge in curriculum so that students are neither bored nor overwhelmed. The inability to find that balance can lead to an inability to learn.

DID YOU KNOW?

Relaxed Alertness

Stress can cause us to shut down, withdraw, or even become agitated or irritable. We have all been there at some point in our lives, and chances are that some of our students have felt this way in our classrooms. In recent years, researchers Renate N. Caine and Geoffrey Caine have described a state, similar to Vygotsky's ZPD, where stress is not present in students' learning environment.

They advocate for educational experiences that provide support and challenge, so that learning is of *moderate challenge*, encouraging a state of "relaxed alertness."[5] The next time a student in your class looks stressed, think about how you can scaffold the experience so that it becomes moderately challenging instead of stressful.

Lev S. Vygotsky's concept of the Zone of Proximal Development (ZPD)[4] is a great example of how brain-based theory can lead to the practice of effectual instructional strategies such as scaffolding.

The Zone of Proximal Development is best described through an event that occurred in my classroom. Have you ever had a student cry, act out, or give up in your classroom because the task that you were asking him or her to accomplish was so difficult that the student just felt like he or she couldn't do it? I have! This is where understanding the ZPD is really important. We each have things that we can accomplish very easily as well as things that we cannot even imagine how to start, or things that we are afraid that we will fail at horribly if we try.

The latter was the case with a girl in my class named Shannon. She was so afraid of art that when I asked the students in my class to look at and sketch the still-life objects at their tables, her face slowly became red, her eyes teary, and she said that she wasn't feeling well. I did not know about her fear of art and, specifically, drawing.

If I had known, I could have broken down, or scaffolded, the lesson to help her accomplish smaller tasks, such as finding the basic shapes in the still life and sketching them, and then adding shadows, then adding details. This would have built her confidence and made the final goal of a completed drawing more attainable for her; but since I didn't know, I assumed she would begin drawing like all the other students had. I had not created the right educational opportunity for Shannon that challenged her enough to help her grow, while ensuring that the task was not too overwhelming to begin.

THEORIES & TERMS

Scaffolding

Scaffolding is an instructional tool that assists teachers in providing adequate support for learners when a new topic is being introduced. Since students will always have varied levels of interest in and knowledge of topics, scaffolding provides a way for all students to engage in a topic at levels of appropriate challenge. This tool provides just enough assistance or support to help students move forward with confidence and greater levels of independence, resulting in the ability to face more complex tasks.

The following strategies can be used to help you scaffold a lesson:

- Recalling or activating prior knowledge.
- Pre-assessing students to gain a better understanding about what they know and to what depth, so that you can design varied entry points through which to engage in a topic at an appropriate level of challenge.
- Breaking complex tasks into chunks or smaller steps to help students build from lower to higher levels of complexity.
- Modeling the process of solving a problem or thinking through the steps needed to accomplish a task.
- Utilizing graphic organizers as a way to help students organize their thoughts and ideas about a topic.

Example Scenario:

The first day of a new unit on comic-book art, I held up a comic book and asked students to tell me everything they knew about comic books, including how they are created. This initial brainstorming allowed us to list collective knowledge that was heard by all students. It helped students recall knowledge they learned in art class the prior year, and provided an opportunity for those who knew more to expand the group's knowledge. In doing this, all students, even those who thought they knew nothing, walked away informed.

After the brainstorming session, each student took a pretest to show me what skills and techniques they knew or remembered about using pen and ink, which would be the primary medium used for the project. This pretest helped me design the lesson for the next class session. Some students knew four of the six techniques, while others knew only one out of six. I then designed three levels of tasks for the next class.

I gave the most knowledgeable group of students the task of trying out two new techniques and then creating their own ideas of how to add texture to their drawings. The middle group had four new techniques to try out. The group that had not used pen and ink before were at a table with me, so I could demonstrate techniques and show them some tips to get started. All groups were given the opportunity to join the demonstration table as a refresher if they decided they needed it.

DID YOU KNOW?

Memory Retention

The first known research study on memory retention was completed in 1885 by Herman Ebbinghaus. He suggested that knowledge related to or associated with existing networks of knowledge has a better chance of storage and recall than unassociated information.[7] Sound familiar? It is the basis for work by Jerome Bruner and for instructional ideas such as the scaffolding and spiraling of knowledge.

The ZPD is the point of equilibrium where students are appropriately challenged by the work they have, not bored because it is too easy or paralyzed because it is too difficult. This is when learning occurs.

Similar to scaffolding, and also commonly used in differentiation, is spiraling. The research of Jerome Bruner and his *Toward a Theory of Instruction* suggest that learning is an *active process* through which learners assemble new ideas or concepts based upon their current and past knowledge.[6] From Bruner's ideas came the concept of spiraling knowledge, in which the introduction of new knowledge connects and builds on prior knowledge.

We do this in our classrooms each time we teach a concept and then refer to it in another related lesson as a way to connect that prior knowledge to new knowledge. This is effective because, through brain research, we know that the brain seeks connections when it stores information. It helps students connect new information to old information and stores it collectively, which makes it more likely that students can recall it.

Instructional Theories

The influence of Vygotsky's and Dewey's work continues to have significant effect on how educators think about and design instruction. Their work lead Bruner to publish his suggestions for the essential features of instruction, containing the following elements:

1 Experiences that excite students and make them want to learn.

2 Information that is taught in ways that learners can easily grasp.

3 An effective sequencing of instruction in an order that makes sense to students.

THEORIES & TERMS

Spiraling

Spiraling is an approach to curriculum planning that helps teachers design strong learning experiences by connecting new information to prior knowledge about the same topic or idea. Why would this be important? When new information is learned, it is stored in the brain in one of two ways: randomly or in connection with prior related knowledge. The strength of spiraling is that it fosters a brain-friendly environment where students, using connections, are more likely to retain and recall new knowledge.

Example Scenario:

At the high school and middle school levels, I have taught students various ways to measure or calculate proportions. During one class, I demonstrated to a group of students how to use a finger as a tool of measure. In the next class, I wanted to teach students another drawing tip, so I asked them as a group to recall and share the tips they already knew about proportions. Then I showed them how to use facial features to approximate proportions when drawing faces. This accomplished two goals: Students recalled prior knowledge so that we could add to it; and it refreshed the memories of those who had forgotten the information. This prepared the group to learn a new fact about proportion to add to their accumulated knowledge.

Tips for Spiraling

- Ask a student or students a question to help them recall older information before sharing something new that relates to it.
- Create curriculum lessons that build on each other, so that the skills learned in the first lesson are used and referred to in the next lesson.
- If you have students over a period of years, build curriculum that spirals from year to year, such as a lesson on weaving in which students learn the basics of weaving with paper one year, weaving with yarn and cloth the next, and weaving with reeds in-the-round the third year.

These elements inform differentiation by calling for instruction that matches the needs of a student's preferences, learning style, and readiness. They also address the need to organize instructional knowledge in a sequential manner to promote learning and acquisition of knowledge, while calling for teachers to consider student interests as a method for designing instruction and as a way to increase student engagement in learning. When interests are used as a hook for learning, student engagement and motivation increases and learning becomes more rewarding and fun.

Learning Theories

Since the 1980s, the amount of knowledge that we have gained in the field of education about how students learn has increased greatly. Prior to that, it was believed that knowledge was finite or fixed and that each person had a predetermined amount of intelligence that he or she could not stretch or increase. This fixed view of intelligence was used to stratify social classes, to track students, and in some cases, to segregate people into groups of individuals deemed worthy of an education and those who were not.

The idea of a fixed intelligence was challenged by researcher Howard Gardner whose work led him to believe that knowledge is fluid, not fixed, and that all people have the capacity to solve problems, learn, and grow. He also challenged the idea that there is only one type or sphere of intelligence, but rather multiple types of intelligence within the brain.

DID YOU KNOW?

Motivation

Have you ever struggled to motivate your students? Consider this: In her work, brain researcher Teresa Amabile noted that intrinsic motivation increased when students were engaged in learning that encouraged them to pursue their interests.[8]

The use of interest-based learning, one of the many strategies that comprise DI, helps students discover and pursue their passions while maximizing their engagement in learning, thereby increasing their productivity. The next time you need to motivate students in a lesson, try to hook them by using their interests.

MAJOR POINTS

Intelligence

All people are intelligent and have the capacity to increase their intelligence. In fact, we all have intelligence in the following areas: verbal/linguistic, logical/mathematical, visual/spatial, bodily/kinesthetic, musical/rhythmical, naturalistic/environmental, interpersonal, and intrapersonal.

THINK POINT

Shaping the Brain

In his book, *Enriching the Brain*, educator Eric Jensen pointed out that not only is the brain's capacity to learn not fixed, but that we now understand that half of what makes us who we are is the result of genetics and half is the result of our unique physical, social, and emotional environments.[9]

Whether you work in your own space or a shared space, take a moment and think about what type of physical, social, and emotional environment exists in your art classroom. What elements foster a safe place for learning to occur? Are there elements that cause stress or limit your students' capacity to work to their best abilities?

Multiple Intelligences Theory

For centuries, teachers have known that students learn differently. It is readily apparent that some students excel at writing, others at solving mathematical problems or creating sculptures. It is this idea of different types of learning that became more refined through Howard Gardner's research. He began to look at intelligence and, with specific criteria in mind, tried to define intelligence in a way that would help to recognize and comprehend the perceived differences about how people learn. This work became known as the "theory of multiple intelligences," one of the core theories that inform Differentiated Instruction.[10]

According to Gardner, the theory of multiple intelligences embodies the concept that intelligence is not singular, but that all people have several discrete areas of intelligence with preferred modes of thinking and working through concepts that vary between individuals. This explains why some students excel in certain areas or readily engage in certain types of learning, but are not as proficient in other areas. He defined eight areas of intelligence: verbal/linguistic, logical/mathematical, visual/spatial, bodily/kinesthetic, musical/rhythmical, naturalistic/environmental, interpersonal, and intrapersonal, with a possible ninth area, existential, that is still debated by educators and researchers.

THEORIES & TERMS

Howard Gardner and the Theory of Multiple Intelligences (MI)

In 1983, Howard Gardner published *Frames of Mind*. This book radically challenged the leading view of intelligence at the time, which stated that there is one type of intelligence and it is fixed, meaning that the level of intelligence with which you were born could not change. The ideas he published in this book, the first of many publications documenting his research, would later be known as the theory of multiple intelligences.

Over time, Gardner defined eight areas of intelligence, which other educators have retitled to help younger children understand themselves and the many ways in which they are smart:

- **Verbal/Linguistic (Word Smart)** This person excels with spoken or written words. He or she often has the capacity to persuade others through stories, speeches, books, poems, or other writings. This intelligence category includes people who are storytellers, politicians, motivational speakers, journalists, poets, editors, and novelists.
- **Logical/Mathematical (Number/Logic Smart)** This person can problem-solve and use numbers proficiently. He or she uses reason and logic to help think through issues. A person with this intelligence might be a scientist, mathematician, accountant, quilter, or computer programmer.
- **Visual/Spatial (Picture Smart)** This person is highly attuned to elements such as space, shape, form, color, and line, and how these elements interact and combine. He or she has the ability to visualize a place, space, or object and then create visual representations of these ideas. People in this group are also aware of the details of the space and the objects around them, noticing aspects and traits that others may not. A person with this intelligence might be a designer, architect, artist, inventor, wilderness guide, or hunter.
- **Bodily/Kinesthetic (Body Smart)** This person is an expert in how he or she moves the body. This intelligence could include dexterity, strength, flexibility, coordination, and balance, as well as the ability to express ideas and emotions through physical movement. It also includes a person who can use his or her hands skillfully to complete tasks, such as an eye surgeon or sculptor. This intelligence category includes, but is not limited to, people who are athletes, dancers, skaters, craftspeople, or mechanics.
- **Musical/Rhythmical (Music Smart)** This person is sensitive to elements of music including rhythm, tone, pitch, and melody. He or she often has what is called an "ear for music," or might be someone who is described as having perfect pitch. This person has a great capacity to perceive, create, and express him- or herself through music. This category of intelligence includes people who are musicians, opera singers, music critics, conductors, performers, and composers.

continued on next page

- **Naturalistic Intelligence (Nature Smart)** This person loves nature and animals. He or she also has a knack for collecting and organizing items. This person would rather be outside in nature than inside. A person with this intelligence might be a shell collector, a veterinarian, or involved in protecting the environment.
- **Intrapersonal (Self Smart)** This person has a strong understanding of him- or herself—his or her strengths, weaknesses, abilities, and needs. Often a person with this type of intelligence is self-assured and attuned to his or her own thoughts.
- **Interpersonal (People Smart)** This person is an expert at relating to other people. He or she has a heightened sensitivity and ability to perceive the moods, intentions, motivations, and feelings of others. He or she is usually very perceptive and often wants to help others. Individuals with this intelligence are considered to be "good with people."

Take a look at your students. Can you think of one who has strong verbal/linguistic intelligence and could talk his or her way out of just about any situation? How about a musical/rhythmical student who hums or taps while working? Try and identify each of the eight intelligence areas by considering your own students. Think of a way to use these natural strengths to hook them into learning in your next lesson.

Gardner's theory has strengthened educational practices and helped educators and students recognize and value differences, instead of devaluing those individuals who do not fit the norm. His model enables teachers to identify their students' intelligence strengths and challenge areas, and empowers teachers and students to use that knowledge to improve performance in challenge areas while building upon their strengths.

This approach emphasizes that *all students are intelligent* and valuable, a message that is powerful for a student to hear. This belief disputes the idea that intelligence is fixed, and it suggests that anyone can learn and grow in knowledge. It also motivates educators to make adequate changes in methods that will enable them to teach and reach their students in new ways. Taking into consideration the preferences that exist

THINK POINT

Does One Size Fit All?

Children already know that they learn differently; just ask them. They can tell who the "artist" is in the class, they can tell you who is good at math, who is a great speller, and which friend will listen to them and give good advice.

Think of instruction as a coat that we, as teachers, are trying to put on our students. Just because students might be of similar age or in a certain grade, does that mean they will all fit into the same size coat? Of course not!

Education, just like a good coat, needs to fit a specific learner; otherwise, a student might feel lost in a coat that is too big, or constricted in a coat that is too small and doesn't allow for growth. Having the wrong size coat, or educational experience, can be embarrassing for students because it makes them look silly and can call attention to their flaws.[11]

within each student offers educators opportunities to stimulate and expand all modes of intelligence beyond their existing parameters. Gardner's research supports the idea that a "one-size-fits-all" approach to education cannot possibly engage all students when their unique needs, strengths, weaknesses, and ideal modes of learning are not considered.

Learning and Thinking Style Profiles

The multiple intelligences theory helps us understand the types of intelligence areas in which students have strengths, but it doesn't necessarily define what teaching methods these students need to help them succeed. For this reason, differentiation also draws from the information that learning- and thinking-style profiles can provide about how students learn best.

An effective way to find out what your students' learning and thinking styles are is to have them fill out an inventory. In a classroom, inventories, such as interest inventories, help teachers collect information about their students, so that they may:

1. Get to know students better.
2. Use the information to design lesson content.
3. Choose big ideas that will best connect with their students.
4. Discover pertinent personal information that a student might wish to share.

TRY THIS

Elementary—One Size Does Not Fit ALL.

With DI, teachers often worry about what students will think if they give various options to different students within their class. Here is a way to help students visualize the concept and begin to understand that you will give each of them exactly what they need to learn and grow, even if it is different from what you give someone else in the room.

Place three coats of various sizes in a pile: one very large, one very small, and one that is average in size. You can even have your students bring their coats to class one day to help you with this activity. Have the smallest child in the class put on the largest coat, have a child put on his or her own coat, and then you, the teacher, try to put on the tiniest coat you can find. Ham it up! Next, ask students, "What's wrong with this picture?" They will notice.

Ask them if they think the same coat would fit each of us. No, of course not; each of us needs a coat that fits us perfectly. Let students know that, similar to the different-sized coats they wear, they all learn differently and have specific and unique things that they need to help them learn. Therefore, you will be fair to all of them by giving them whatever they may need to best learn in art class.

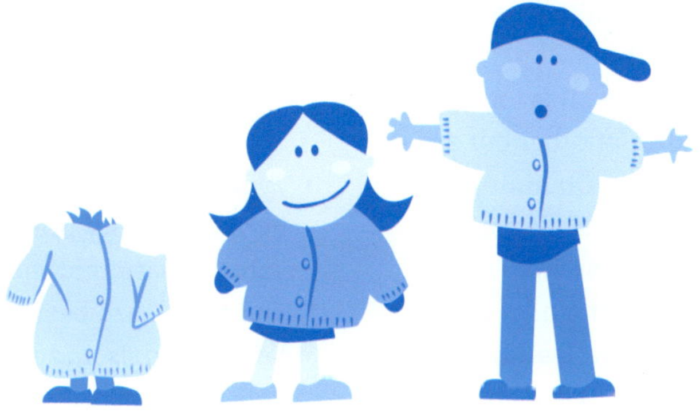

2.2 One Coat Does Not Fit All. Designed by Carrie Miller.

There are many inventories of these profiles, but two are more commonly used than others—those developed by Bernice McCarthy and Robert J. Sternberg. You will note some similarities between the two, but each uses different words or descriptions to accomplish the same goal, which is to help define how learners access and process information in unique and individual ways.

THEORIES & TERMS

Bernice McCarthy's 4MAT Model

The 4MAT (a play on the word "format") model, an instructional design tool, is based on the interplay between how people perceive and then process what they perceive. It was developed with the notion that all students will need to move through a learning cycle in order to achieve understanding, including areas they are not very comfortable with.

McCarthy suggested that we all favor one particular learning style over another but are capable of working in all areas. Obtaining this information about your students' learning styles is important because it can help them understand how they learn best, and it can help you understand and design lessons that incorporate strategies that engage all four types of learners.

This tool helps identify and understand the needs of four types of learners:[12]

- **Type I Imaginative Learner** These students need to see how the learning is meaningful to them and that there is a reason for them to learn it. They learn best through watching, reflecting, and connecting with their feelings, and they tend to be innovative. They might wonder or ask, "Why?"
- **Type II Analytical Learner** Listening to and thinking about information is the prime mode of learning for students with this style. They like facts, thinking through ideas, and finding out what an expert thinks through a presentation such as a lecture. They might wonder or ask, "What?"
- **Type III Common Sense Learner** Learners in this category prefer to apply ideas. They value experimentation and problem solving, and they learn best when they can manipulate materials and read directions that provide assistance as a task begins. They might wonder or ask, "How?"
- **Type IV Dynamic Learner** These students learn best through trial and error. They are learners who acquire knowledge though their senses. They are risk-takers and prefer self-discovery and freedom of choice in their learning. They might wonder or ask, "If?"

THEORIES & TERMS

Sternberg's Learning-Style Theory of Intelligence: The Triarchic Theory

Like Howard Gardner, noted psychologist Robert J. Sternberg believed that traditional measures of intelligence only partially capture an accurate measurement of intelligence.[13] Sternberg's research focused on how individuals use their intelligence to deal with changes in their environment, which lead him to believe that three types of learners or categories of intelligence exist: analytical, practical, and creative. He describes the three types of learners as:

- **Analytical/Componential** This type of learner does well in traditional academic environments and is good at test-taking, memorization, and logically ordered thought. Individuals in this group often view concepts or ideas in black and white and have difficulty creating original ideas.
- **Practical/ Contextual** This type of learner has what Sternberg calls "street smarts" and is adept at using experience to guide the decision-making process. These learners seem to fit in any situation and are able to use the contextual information around them to "figure out" what they need to do to succeed.
- **Creative/Experiential** This type of learner is able to manage a novel situation well, generates new ideas, creates solutions, tests theories, and thinks outside the box.

Although this theory categorizes learners using different titles, there is clearly a significant overlap between Sternberg's theory and the 4MAT model. Similar to McCarthy, Sternberg acknowledges that all individuals possess an integration of all three types of intelligence, but often favor one over another.

THEORIES & TERMS

The Four Square Model: Understanding Student Learning Styles

My favorite learning-style inventory, the four square model, is a straightforward combination of the learning-style theories considered in this chapter. This format defines types of learners in ways that students find easy to relate to and use. It defines four types of learners: visual, kinesthetic, auditory, and written.

Visual

- Needs to see a picture or example to understand.
- Drawn to colors and visually appealing objects.
- Prefers books with illustrations.
- Appears to be daydreaming but is trying to acquire a visual picture of what is being said.
- Remembers better when can see the person speaking.
- Explains by drawing illustrations of the concept they are explaining.

Kinesthetic

- Learns best by physically participating in a task.
- Difficulty staying still for more than a few minutes.
- Often ignores directions and begins to figure out the task independently.
- Almost always has some body part in motion.
- Prefers to hear or read stories that are full of action.
- Needs to make, do, or work through a process.

Written

- Needs to write out information in order to process what is being learned.
- Often is quiet and introverted.
- Likes to take notes and collect written material.
- Benefits from conducting research.
- Enjoys using the Internet to discover and read.
- Benefits from project, behavioral, or task directions being posted.

Auditory

- Needs to hear it to remember it.
- Often needs to talk through what they are thinking in order to understand it themselves.
- Memorizes best by repeating aloud or to oneself what is being said.
- Remembers best when facts or information is learned through mnemonic, rhythmic, or musical methods.
- Prefers to listen to a book.

2.3 *Four Square Learning.* Graphic designed by Heather L. R. Fountain.

Younger students, students who are nonverbal, or students who struggle with English can also create inventories by drawing, writing, or collecting images of things they like and adding them on a paper shape that contains their name. These inventories can be placed along the top edge of the wall in the classroom so that students can see themselves as part of the classroom community. Their chosen images can also be used for activities such as compare and contrast, finding a partner with a similar interest, or to graph common interests of the class.

Conclusion

Each theory and practice that informs DI helps to create a unified instructional practice that values all types of learners. Brain research and instructional theories help teachers understand how to design lessons that help all students connect to the subject matter and successfully process and store the information. Multiple intelligences and learning-style theories inform learners and teachers of the various unique learning strengths that exist. Armed with this information, students can begin to understand and value not only their similarities, but also their differences and recognize them as strengths not weaknesses.

This concept is vital to the art classroom where it begins to build students' confidence in their abilities. It helps them understand that they can access art in many ways, and that it is acceptable for one person to be excellent at sculpting, while another might excel in talking about art's aesthetic properties. These theories do not inform the topics that are taught in the classroom, but rather they help teachers decide how, why, and when to teach particular subjects and who will teach them—students or teachers.

REFLECTION & PRACTICE

Understanding Learners

1 **Learning Styles** Take a moment to consider what type of learner you are by looking at the following learning-style theories: 4MAT, MI, Sternberg, and the four square.

What type of learner are you? What are your MI strengths and areas of weakness? How does your learning style affect how you teach your students?

2 **Spiraling** For each grade you teach, make a chart that catalogues the lesson or units in order of occurrence over the course of your year or term together. Once you have your chart created, take a look at two things:

- Are the lessons in an order that build on prior knowledge, or should they be rearranged in a different sequence that better allows students to take new knowledge and connect it to prior experiences?
- If you have students over multiple years or classes, do the lessons from each year or each class carry over into the next, while asking students to draw from prior knowledge and skills and adding to it?

3 **Engagement** What strategies do you use to help struggling learners feel more connected or comfortable with engaging in art? What types of students do you feel that you need help reaching or helping to connect with art?

Notes

1 J. Dewey, *Experience & Education* (New York: MacMillan, 1938).

2 G. Wiggins and J. McTighe, *Understanding by Design* (Alexandria, VA: Association for Supervision and Curriculum Development, 1998).

3 M. G. Stewart and S. R. Walker, *Rethinking Curriculum in Art* (Worcester, MA: Davis Publications, 2005).

4 L. S. Vygotsky, *Thought and Language* (Cambridge, MA: Massachusetts Institute of Technology Press, 1962); L. S. Vygotsky *Mind in Society: The Development of Higher Psychological Processes* (Cambridge, MA: Harvard University Press, 1980).

5 R. N. Caine and G. Caine. *Making Connections: Teaching and the Human Brain* (Alexandria, VA: Association for Supervision and Curriculum and Development, 1991).

6 J. Bruner, *Toward a Theory of Instruction* (Cambridge, MA: Harvard University Press, 1996).

7 P. Wolfe, *Brain Matters: Translating Research into Classroom Practice* (Alexandria, VA: Association for Supervision and Curriculum Development, 2001).

8 T. M. Amabile, *The Social Psychology of Creativity* (New York: Springer-Verlag, 1983); M. A. Collins and T. M. Amabile. "Motivation and Creativity," in R. J. Sternberg, ed., *Handbook of Creativity* (New York: Cambridge University Press, 1999): pp. 297–312.

9 E. Jensen, *Enriching the Brain: How to Maximize Every Learner's Potential* (San Francisco: Jossey-Bass, 2006).

10 H. Gardner, *Frames of Mind: The Theory of Multiple Intelligences*, 10th anniversary ed. (New York: Basic Books, 1993); H. Gardner, *Multiple Intelligences: The Theory in Practice* (New York: Basic Books, 1993); H. Gardner, *Intelligence Reframed: Multiple Intelligences for the 21st Century* (New York: Basic Books, 1999); H. Gardner, *Multiple Intelligences: New Horizons* (New York: Basic Books, 2006).

11 Carol Ann Tomlinson used the coats metaphor in an Advanced DI pre-conference session at the Association for Supervision and Curriculum Development Conference [ASCD]. You can find this presentation and many other resources on her website, http://www.caroltomlinson.com.

12 "Using the 4MAT System to Bring Learning Styles to Schools," *Educational Leadership*, 48, no. 2 (1990): pp. 31–37; B. McCarthy, *About Teaching: 4MAT in the Classroom* (Wanconda, IL: About Learning, 2000).

13 R. J. Sternberg, ed., *The Nature of Creativity: Contemporary Psychological Perspectives* (New York: Cambridge University Press, 1988); R. J. Sternberg and L. A. O'Hara, "Creativity and Intelligence," in R. J. Sternberg, ed., *Handbook of Creativity* (New York: Cambridge University Press, 1999): pp. 251–272; R. J. Sternberg and W. M. Williams, (1996). *How to Develop Student Creativity* (Alexandria, VA: Association for Supervision and Curriculum Development, 1996).

Chapter 3

Why Teach This Way?

"Every truth has four corners: as a teacher I give you one corner, and it is for you to find the other three."

Confucius

PERSONAL CONNECTIONS

Strengthening Practice

As you read, consider the following questions:

1 What are some things that you would like to change or strengthen in your teaching practice?

2 What types of students are motivated in your classroom and what types of students have difficulty being motivated?

3 If you could spend less time on discipline in your class what could you accomplish?

Effects and Benefits

It's Saturday morning and eleven teachers are gathered around a large square table sharing their recent experiences of Differentiated Instruction in their classrooms. The stories shared thus far have been exciting and humorous; the mood is light when Betty suddenly exclaims, "I have a new problem in my room!" Everyone sits up ready to listen and offer advice; she then explains that for the first time in her career, her students want to be in her room all of the time. They are sad to leave at the end of art class and want to be in art during free periods and recess—even the kids who have never liked art before. Other teachers quickly chime in that they are experiencing similar things, too. Wow, kids so excited about art that they can't get enough. Wouldn't that be a delightful problem to have?

This chapter will provide you with research about DI and stories of how it has affected the students and teachers who have experienced it in their classrooms. You will find a combination of perspectives gathered from teachers and students, ranging from elementary through high school.

My Classroom and Research

I have always been very curious. I was the kind of child who asked many questions such as "Why?" and "What if...?" My wish in third grade was for a microscope so I could discover the answers to mysteries around me that I could not perceive with my eyes alone. I had to know more. This same desire led me to wonder about my own teaching and my own classroom. I loved my school and teaching my students, but I wanted to achieve a higher level of understanding. Specifically, I wanted to know if what I saw happening in my classroom—students excited and

PERSPECTIVES

Differentiated Instruction and Motivation

"I honestly believe that DI has heightened my students' interest and retention, and it allows them to participate in ways that help them find meaning in their lessons, as well as a sense of success." Paraprofessional

"The students were so excited! I have never had a project where I reached everyone in the room. I offered them three choices; the students instantly decided which choice was right for them. At the end of the class, students looked so disappointed because they had to stop working on their ideas." High School Art Educator

"While teaching the differentiated lessons I planned for my art classroom, I noticed that kids were more engaged in the projects than they had been in previous lessons. They were showing a deeper understanding of what they were doing. Students even began to ask to come to the artroom when they did not have art, to work on their projects, even those students who usually only did the bare minimum." Middle School Art Educator

engaged in art learning—could happen in other classrooms. I also wanted to know if this was happening because I was using DI or if there was another reason.

I witnessed how my school and classroom thrived with the use of DI. Even students who were not "into school" or not "into art" became excited to be in the artroom. Students in my classes became more engaged, more knowledgeable, more capable, and more respectful of each other as I became more facile in differentiating. These attributes enabled me to create a quality art program that exceeded expectations and made my administration, parents, and students proud of the accomplishments that were happening in the artroom.

Despite the positive feedback, I still felt an obligation to other teachers in my field and to myself; I needed to go beyond my own classroom and school and into the arena of research and doctoral studies.

For half a year, I worked as a consultant in an elementary school and collected data on how student learning was positively affected by the use of Differentiated Instruction. I began to notice that students were making more choices on their own, problem-solving, relying on each other as experts in different subjects, and achieving greater gains in learning than they had before. A first grade teacher was amazed at how much more engaged her students were, even in writing, which many had avoided in the past. Even parents noticed how excited their children had become about what they were learning. If such important changes could be seen in a relatively short amount of time, I wondered what I would find if I spent a whole school year collecting data about Differentiated Instruction.

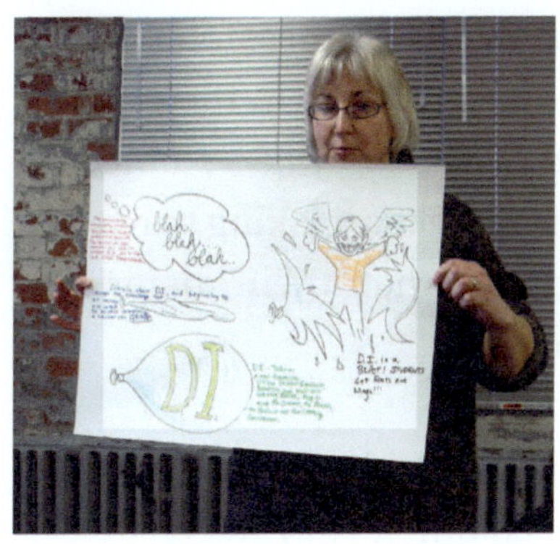

3.1 Anne shares with her colleagues how DI has transformed her teaching, helping her students burst from "blah blah blah" into life. In her words, DI has helped to give her students "wings." Photo by Heather L. R. Fountain.

The next school year, I continued my research into the effects of DI on student learning in another school. I observed, interviewed, and documented the progress of one classroom teacher as she began to use art to differentiate instruction in her classroom of third and fourth graders. I was interested to see if I would find results similar to those I had found in my own classroom. I focused specifically on how the use of art to differentiate instruction affected the social, emotional, and physical environment of the classroom and if the implementation of DI would promote an increase in creative-thinking skills.

At the end of the year, after analyzing the data I had collected, it became clear that the teacher and students in this classroom experienced significant benefits by the use of DI. Differentiated Instruction had helped both teacher and students transform their classroom into a place where all students were important, felt safe having and expressing opinions, and were willing to take risks, even if they risked failure. Students' sense of ownership of the classroom space and their learning extended to changes in the physical space of the room as well.

3.2 As students valued their work and took more ownership of the room, they requested a special place to display their work. With a lack of space in the room for display, the custodian helped them create a gallery space by hanging a string across the room. Photo by Heather L. R. Fountain.

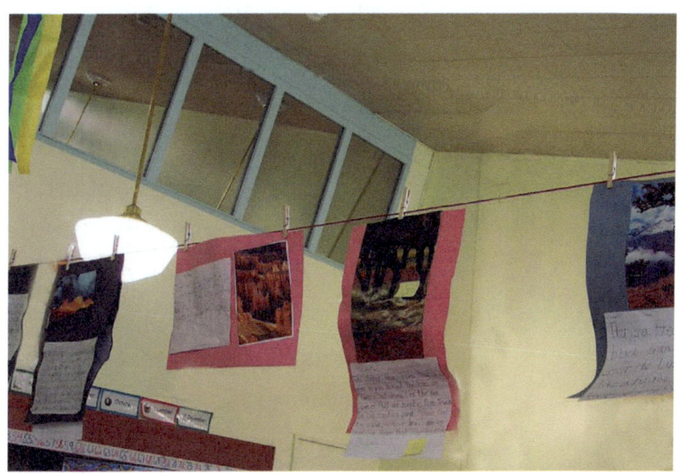

PERSPECTIVES

Differentiated Instruction and the Classroom Environment

"I have found that when you watch students in a differentiated classroom, you observe a level of excitement and an engagement in learning that is far more intense than that of a non-differentiated environment." Elementary Art Educator

Students made plans for the innovative use of classroom and hallway space, and even asked for special places in the room to display their artwork or works by the artist they had studied. They also took better care of the art supplies, making sure to return them to their proper locations, so that "their" materials would be there when needed again.

From a social perspective, the students in this classroom appeared to be comfortable with each other. They freely discussed both school-related and personal topics. They solicited each other's ideas and assistance, and accepted each other's strengths and weaknesses. The students took responsibility for each other and helped each other accomplish tasks.

The level of creativity that students expressed also seemed to be affected by the use of DI. Students in third and fourth grade typically begin to doubt their abilities in art and quite often start hiding their work or have less interest in or greater fear of engaging in art-making. Some researchers have called this the U-curve of artistic development, a time when most students' creative expression begins to stagnate or diminish.[1]

The opposite was happening for these students. They reported feeling more creative at the end of the school year. Their reasons for their increased creativity fit within two main categories: some felt that they were more creative because they had learned a lot about art; others said it was because they had been given more opportunities to make decisions and to be more creative than ever before.

I thought it was great that an entire class of students felt that they were more creative at the end of one school year, but were they? Fortunately, I had tested each student at the beginning and end of the school year using a creative-thinking inventory.[1] After analyzing the creative-thinking tests that measured each student's creative-thinking skills, I saw that every student in this class did indeed have some increase in his or her ability to think creatively. One might think that this would be expected, as we should be more creative each year as we learn more, but it is not typically the case. This is the opposite of what most studies have found at the end of a school year for third and fourth graders in a traditional school setting.

Benefits for Students

Learning occurs best for students in an environment that contains positive interpersonal relationships and interactions, as well as comfort and order, and in which the learner feels appreciated, acknowledged, respected, and validated.[2] DI has been shown to help foster a classroom environment in which these attributes exist. Students in these classrooms have often been found to be more engaged in learning, to work harder, to have greater learning gains, to exhibit more positive behaviors, and to build stronger student and teacher relationships.

Positive Behavior

"And I would argue the second greatest force in the universe is ownership." Chris Chocola

Teachers who use DI consistently have found that the incidence of student disciplinary issues greatly decreases, allowing both students and teachers to spend their class time more meaningfully. I found this to be true especially when I took steps to foster student ownership in my classroom.

At the beginning of each school year, I asked students what conditions they needed in order to have a safe art classroom

PERSPECTIVES

Differentiated Instruction and Classroom Management

"My students were so excited to have choices and be able to decide how they wanted to complete a part of their project that they [remained] engaged, stayed on task, and focused. This gave me more time to walk around and talk with them, instead of spending that time policing or dealing with classroom management." High School Integrated Arts Educator

"I like that I get to make decisions and be treated like an adult." High School Student

"When students are engaged and excited about what they are doing, they have no time to mess around." Justin, Elementary Art Educator

where they would feel comfortable. Each class of students in every grade created a list of important items. The lists were almost identical for every class. Additionally, I found that my students included all of the expectations I would have listed myself. I took all of their ideas and combined them into one list for them to vote on. It may seem quicker to post a list of teacher-created rules, but I found the opposite to be true.

When I posted a list of rules, they were my rules and I was in charge of enforcing them. They were rules that, from many of my students' perspectives, I was imposing on them. But when students created the rules and voted on them, the rules were theirs and they were responsible for following and enforcing them. I was amazed how one class period could set a positive tone for the entire school year. In addition, I heard students reminding each other of the rules and letting people know what was expected in their classroom. On occasions when I saw students making poor choices, I would remind them to read the list they voted on and make a better choice. Rarely did I have to discipline students with more than a reminder.

When given an opportunity, students will step up and take part in running their classroom. Whether helping other students, holding each other accountable, or participating in classroom activities, actively contributing to a community and being valued by that community is powerful. This idea of being part of a team also reduces selfishness, as students see how their actions affect their ability to use or not use certain materials, participate in interactive learning, and engage in discussion.

DI helps teachers foster an environment of respect in which students' voices and ideas are valued, and it extends the notion of leadership to include students as important members of a team. This sense of leadership continues to grow and evolve as students are provided opportunities to make decisions and take responsibility for their behaviors and learning goals; the definition of leadership widens to include every member of the class, instead of a chosen few.

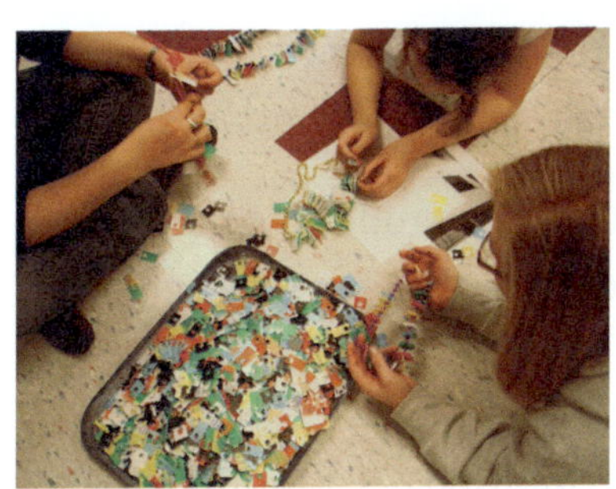

3.3 With fewer behavioral issues to address in the classroom, students can accomplish greater things, such as the use of special media or unique learning experiences outside the classroom. Here, students work in a team to create an installation piece for a local building. Photo by Heather L. R. Fountain.

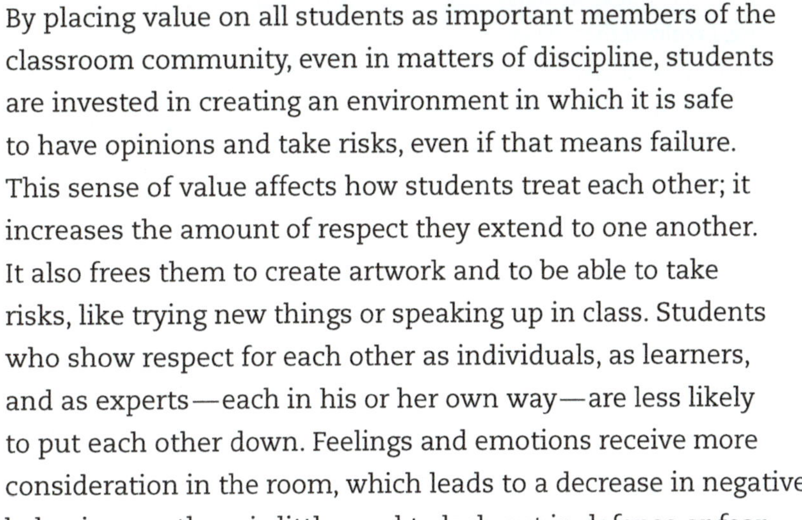

By placing value on all students as important members of the classroom community, even in matters of discipline, students are invested in creating an environment in which it is safe to have opinions and take risks, even if that means failure. This sense of value affects how students treat each other; it increases the amount of respect they extend to one another. It also frees them to create artwork and to be able to take risks, like trying new things or speaking up in class. Students who show respect for each other as individuals, as learners, and as experts—each in his or her own way—are less likely to put each other down. Feelings and emotions receive more consideration in the room, which leads to a decrease in negative behaviors, as there is little need to lash out in defense or fear.

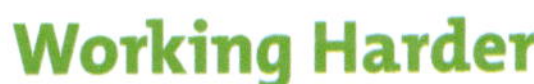

Working Harder

"Find something you love to do and you'll never have to work a day in your life." Harvey MacKay

Differentiated Instruction consists of best-practice strategies that help teachers connect students with learning in ways that often make it seem less like work. Through the design of instruction that includes choice-based options, interest-related connections, or carefully matched levels of inquiry, DI helps students become so invested in their learning that they often perceive their work as easier, when in fact they are usually working harder. If you have ever been excited about a topic or an artwork you were creating and lost track of time, you

PERSPECTIVES

Differentiated Instruction and Reaching Students

"At first I was hesitant because it seemed like a lot of extra work. As I learned to put some things into practice, I realized that the extra work was worth it and it's even fun. Students are interested and engaged in lessons, empowered, and appropriately challenged." Student Teacher

"Kids were more engaged in the projects than they had been in previous lessons. Each child was showing deeper understanding of what he or she was doing. Students were going above and beyond my requirements. They were interested, engaged, and they far surpassed my wildest expectations. All this excitement makes me want to teach this way all the time. This means a lot more time will be involved in planning, but the final outcome of the process would be more than worth the initial effort on my part. More than [at any time in] the last five years, I am now truly excited about my job." Middle School Art Educator

can understand this perception. It is easier to work on things that we like and can connect to, than on things we perceive as unimportant or unrelated to our lives. This positive shift in perception happens for the following reasons:

1 Students often have some choice in what they are working on, which builds ownership.

2 Students' interests are used to help build motivation.

3 Personal connections are made between students and the topic that build personal investment in the success of the project.

After a year of research at the elementary level, I found that most students described their year of using DI as easier. When I asked them why it was easier, they told me that they had fun and enjoyed what they had done. Their teacher elaborated on this by adding that students who usually struggled were able to connect with the content in new ways, which led to less frustration and a greater amount of learning.

It wasn't only the elementary students who were experiencing success. After working with a graduate student on a research project that documented the process of using DI in a high school art class, we found similar results. The high school students were interviewed about the use of DI in their art class. Their perceptions of learning when DI was used were as follows:

- It's easier and you feel a lot more comfortable and confident.
- It's a lot easier. It's so much better.
- It's easier because we get to make choices and decide what we do.

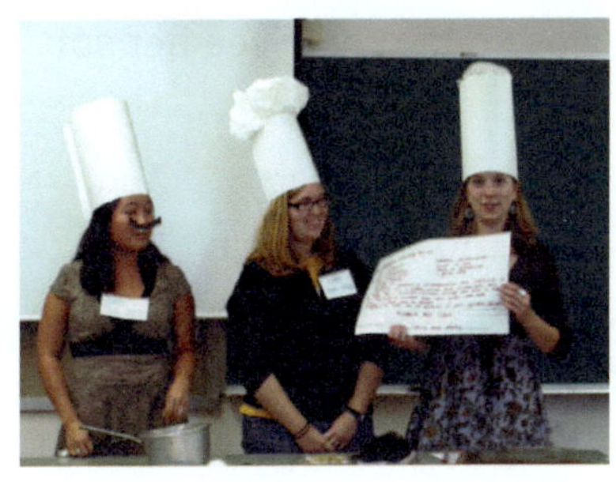

3.4 Giving students the opportunity to make decisions about their learning creates an environment in which they feel valued and confident. Students choose to perform a cooking show to demonstrate the ingredients for a safe classroom. Photo by Heater L. R. Fountain.

In this classroom situation, students did not waste time and even complained when class was over. They were invested in the project and were busy working throughout the entire period. The art teacher for this high school class, Addy McKerns, commented that the students in the DI classroom had accomplished more than those who had been involved with this lesson in a conventional class environment the year before. Although both groups had the same objectives, she had modified the lesson to add choice and personal connection, which had a great impact on how hard the groups worked to accomplish their projects. She noted excitedly that students came to each class eager to be in the room and focused solely on their projects.

Engagement in Learning

Learning becomes attainable and exciting when we design curriculum in a way that helps all students connect with its content in different ways that meet their learning needs. This excitement can lead to greater levels of engagement and enjoyment in learning.

A perfect example of this happened one day while I was conducting research in Massachusetts. Students were working enthusiastically on projects that they had chosen from several options posted by their teacher; their interest was so great that it made its way home to many of their parents.

During that week alone, several mothers shared with the teacher and me that their children were so excited about the projects they were working on that they had been talking about them at home. One mother asked to speak to me alone; she wanted me to know that her son, who usually was not enthusiastic about school, came home inspired by the activities

PERSPECTIVES

Differentiated Instruction and Engagement

"My students are more invested in their work when I offer them choices in projects. They are also more receptive to working in groups when I group them with other students who share their strongest intelligences. I have found even the non-artist individuals are more interested and willing to become involved in learning than they may have been previously." Middle School Art Educator

"I have never seen my students as confident and engaged in their learning as when I differentiate my instruction." Elementary Art Educator

"Since incorporating DI into my daily teaching practices, I have found that my students are much more receptive to learning about art. The students enjoy what they are doing and like how they are learning about it. As an educator, this has been a wonderful breakthrough for me." Middle School Art Educator

"DI is like a wildfire! I am excited, my students are excited, and other teachers are starting to notice, too." Elementary Art Educator

going on in the art classroom. She was so happy to see her son finally loving school!

It is fairly common for students—even those who don't like school—to feel more positive about class and even about school in general when they experience DI. A graduate student of mine who had recently begun to employ DI in her middle-school artroom explained that at first, she questioned the extra time it took to prepare her differentiated lessons, but soon realized that differentiation was well worth the time because her students had become highly interested and engaged, "even the kids who *hated* art." To her surprise, some students even asked for extra work to do on the topics they were studying.

Benefits for Teachers

"When love and skill work together, expect a masterpiece."
John Ruskin

A principal proudly led a group of school board members through the hallway, stopping in the doorway of one classroom—the artroom. At first glance, this room might have appeared chaotic from the perspective of an outsider, but the principal saw beyond the commotion and noise to recognize the sights and sounds of a classroom that was alive. She saw students who were not only in school but were also actively engaged in learning and questioning.

The group of board members watched as the students talked animatedly and conferenced together, sharing their artwork and asking the question, "What can I do to make this better?" The board observed the teacher walking from group to group listening in on the banter and interjecting a question when needed to help a group focus in positive directions.

Consider what a powerful message of advocacy this observation communicated to school visitors that day. As a result, those school board members had reason to reevaluate their ideas about education, and they mentioned that they wished their own schooling had been more like what they had observed. Their definition of school was transformed from a place where silence is cherished, desks are in rows, and children are learning by quietly listening and taking notes on what the teacher is saying at the front of the classroom, to an environment where an educator can teach students through interaction and critical thinking while, at the same time, fostering community.

Many of the benefits for students coincide with the benefits teachers have seen as a result of using DI. The relationship between teachers and students in the classroom creates a complex weave of interaction that overlaps and combines in powerful ways.

Time to Connect

"DI is possible in an artroom—it's NOT too difficult and is a tool to actually increase efficiency and allow the art teacher time to engage with his or her students on an individual basis."
Laura, Art Educator

At the end of a conference workshop on DI that I was teaching, an art teacher posed a question to which many teachers can relate. She asked, "I have thirty-five students in a class and six classes a day; how can I ever get to know my students and find the time to use DI?" This was a valid question and as I considered how to answer it I heard another voice. A teacher in the room shared that she had wondered the same thing at first but soon discovered that for her, DI "took more time to plan

PERSPECTIVES

Differentiated Instruction and Connecting with Students

"DI has changed my classroom into a place where students take responsibility for themselves and their work. They also help each other much more than they used to, which allows me the freedom to walk around and interact with my students more." Middle School Art Educator

PERSPECTIVES

DI and Relationships

"I share more with my students about how I teach and how I think, and they know my interests. Their interest in me was a big surprise—how must they feel when I take an interest in them?" Middle School Art Educator

"As you walk around and observe in my room, you see students understanding and appreciating each other's learning styles. A sense of belonging, of having the same way of learning as others prevails, while at the same time, there is a realization that difference is a good thing." Elementary Art Educator

initially, but often allowed me more freedom in my classroom to spend time with students and get to know them or work with them individually." How could this be? Well if you are designing lessons that require your students to make choices and decisions, think critically, problem-solve, and interact with their subject, you will be working smarter, not harder during the class period, as will they.

For instance, you could create a lesson in which students are working at stations to discover various aspects of a style of art they are exploring. At their stations, they have the directions, goals, and items they need to consider, all prepared for them ahead of time. While students work, you are available to circulate through the room, talk with them, check their comprehension and behavior, and ask questions to help groups focus on their task. This freedom will allow you the ability to connect more with students and even find time to accomplish tasks you never dreamed possible, such as holding individual conferences or portfolio reviews with students.

Stronger Relationships with Students

"She's cool and she gets down on our level and it's more relaxed.... She knows me." Dan, High School Student

Relationships take time. As students become more involved in their own learning and begin to take on more responsibility, teachers gain more time to connect with them. It can be as simple as telling and showing them that we believe they are important. One of my students told me that she knew I cared about her because I asked her how she was doing and actually listened. I wondered how she knew that I was "actually listening," so I asked her. She told me that I remembered or noticed things about her such as that she was not feeling well last class or that she had a new haircut. When I mentioned these things, she knew I cared about her. Another way I was able to build stronger connections with my hundreds of students was by pre-assessment of their interests in art and life. This alone showed students that I cared about their ideas, opinions, and interests, but it also helped me design lessons and behavior management plans that connected with my students. The most important things a child wants from his or her teacher, no matter the child's age, is to be acknowledged and liked. It is important to notice our students' work, but it's also important to notice aspects of their lives, both big and small.

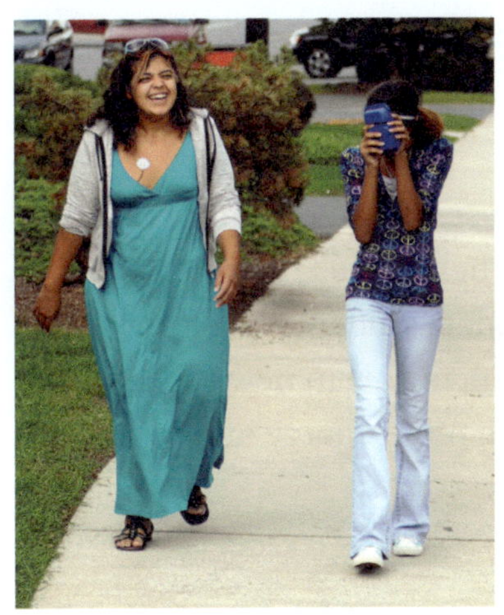

3.5 Getting to know your students and valuing their ideas helps you make deeper, more meaningful connections with them educationally and personally. Photo by Heather L. R. Fountain.

PERSPECTIVES

Differentiated Instruction and Ownership

"In my class, choice cards have helped my students apply what they have learned and they give students ownership of the choices they made." Middle School Art Educator

"I differentiated an old lesson plan that I thought needed some spicing up. In the past, students left their artwork behind, but this time around, NO projects were left behind in my room. They were all so eager to take their creations home." High School Art Educator

More and Deeper Content

"With pre-assessment I found out that my students already knew things I was planning on teaching. This allowed me to move on to other lessons and, in many cases, do things that both they and I were more excited about." Shamika, Middle School Art Educator

There never seems to be enough time. Halfway through each school year, I would always have a mini panic attack thinking of all the things my students and I had not studied yet in the artroom. There are so many artists, artworks, styles, and media to experience, but time is always an issue. With the use of pre-assessment to find out what students already know, you can eliminate some content or cover it in less time. Also, with fewer negative behaviors to manage and less leadership and care of the artroom falling on your shoulders alone, you will have more time to cover more content. I found that using the tools I learned through DI gave me more time to:

- Provide further depth to the art content I was teaching.
- Work with individual students or groups of students who were struggling.

- Work on building stronger lessons and extension activities.
- Cover a greater amount of content.

All of this was accomplished because both the students and I were effectively using our time where it was needed. By not teaching content that was not needed, students were not bored or lost but were effectively experiencing art in new and exciting ways. The students seemed to have more energy and so did I.

Reach More Students

"As I saw DI in action in my own classroom, it became personal for me. [It was] personal because growing up I had trouble in school—I was not the best student. I saw students that reminded me of myself, some of them troublemakers, finding success with this new teaching style." Jess, Middle School Art Educator

Many students feel that art, or even school in general, is not for them; at some point, they have lost interest in learning or confidence in themselves. Through the use of interest-related choices, and tasks that match the level of students' readiness for learning or engagement that utilize their learning styles, students gain confidence in their abilities and find greater connection to learning.

At the end of the school year, the teacher I observed for my research shared with me that she felt that she had reached more students that year by using DI. She saw students coming out of their shells and engaging in learning in ways they had not done in the prior year. She also reflected that the students seemed to have enjoyed their learning more because she designed lessons that fit many of their learning styles and created ownership by building choice into their learning;

students were able to use their strengths to help them reach their learning goals and build up their abilities in their areas of challenge.

Engaging Learning Environments

"DI changes your role and allows you to step back and let students work more, think more, and be more involved in their learning." Diane, Elementary Educator

What is a teacher? The idea of what makes a teacher has changed over time. For some, a teacher is a person who, from the front of the classroom, pours out his or her knowledge for students. With DI, the image of a teacher often shifts from someone who imparts knowledge to someone who provides opportunities and guidance for students to wonder, seek, and discover knowledge authentically. This student-focused process helps them gain ownership of their learning and builds their level of engagement, as well as their ability to recall and remember what they have learned.

One way to shift from a teacher-focused environment is to ask more questions of students and give fewer answers immediately. This process eliminates the situation of learned helplessness in which students constantly ask their teacher for directions or answers, often for things they already know, instead of thinking about them and seeking the answers themselves. By asking more questions, in combination with teaching students strategies for seeking answers, they learn not only how to discover knowledge, but also how to seek it independently from many sources, including their peers. Students are no longer solely dependent on their teacher. Teaching students to think critically and independently gives them skills that will serve them well beyond the classroom.

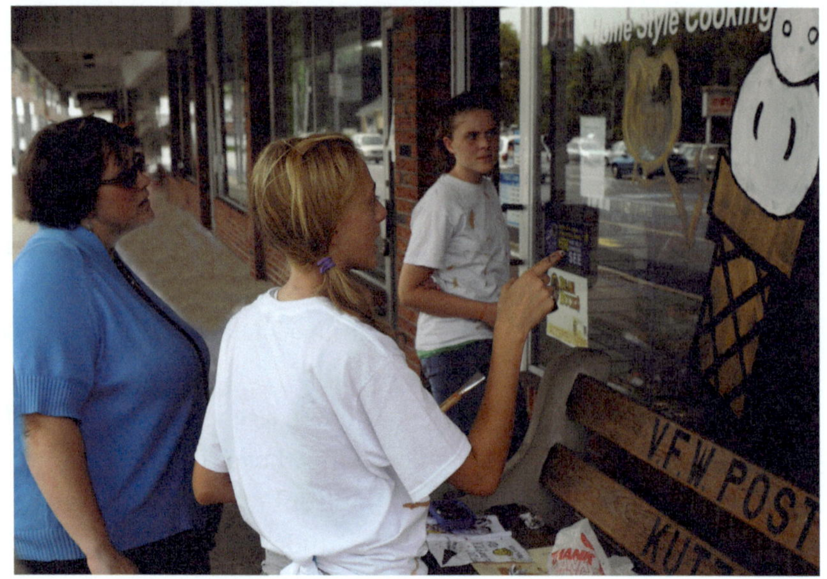

3.6 DI is successful when a teacher recognizes that he or she does not need to provide students with all the answers. Students benefit from learning how to think by problem-solving and discovering the answers for themselves. Photo by Dan Moyer.

PERSPECTIVES

Differentiated Instruction and Flexibility

"I appreciate how there are various ways of differentiating instruction—the whole lesson could be designed around it or just some part. It can be inserted fairly easily." High School Art Educator

MAJOR POINTS

Fostering Community

Differentiated Instruction helps to foster a community in which teachers and students build strong relationships and find meaning, value, and ownership in the learning process.

Conclusion

The benefits of considering and employing DI can be quite extensive for both teachers and students. As a teacher of students ranging from preschool age to adults, using DI has energized, and continues to energize, my practice. It helps me connect my students to ideas in ways that make learning authentic and real for them. It helps me turn my classroom into a safe place where my students are empowered to believe in themselves as leaders and decision-makers.

REFLECTION & PRACTICE

Strengthening Practice

1 **A Problem Like That** In the opening paragraph of this chapter, a teacher describes a "problem" she is having in her classroom; take a moment to dream big and define what problem you wish you had in your classroom.

2 **Motivation** How do you currently help to motivate all your students to be excited about learning? To ramp up student motivation, consider adding a hook, an introductory activity or experience that captures students' attention, at the start of your next class. What could you do to surprise, delight, or capture their attention?

3 **Ownership** This week, reflect on your role as a teacher. What do you define as your job? Where do you situate yourself during the class period? What tasks or responsibilities do you relinquish to students? In what ways do you foster student responsibility and leadership? How much of the time do you give students the answers, opposed to letting them explore or discover them on their own? What tasks do you complete or take care of in the classroom that students should or could be doing? After considering these questions, set one goal for how you can promote your students as leaders and explorers in the classroom.

Notes

1 J. H. Davis, (1991). "Artistry Lost: U-shaped Development in Graphic Symbolization" (doctoral dissertation, Harvard Graduate School of Education, 1991); H. Gardner and E. Winner, "First Intimations of Artistry," in S. Strauss, ed., *U-Shaped Development* (New York: Academic Press, 1982).

2 E. P. Torrance, *Torrance Tests of Creative Thinking* [Updated] (Princeton: 1990); E. P. Torrance, O. E. Ball, and H. T. Safter, *Torrance Test of Creative Thinking: Streamlined Scoring Guide, Figural A and B* (Bensenville, IL: Scholastic Testing Service, 1992); E. P. Torrance and P. A. Haensly, "Assessment of Creativity in Children and Adolescents," in C. R. Reynolds and R. W. Kamphaus, eds., *Handbook of Psychological and Educational Assessment of Children: Intelligence and Achievement* (New York: Guilford, 1990): pp. 697–719.

3 N. M. Lambert and B. L. McCombs, eds. (1998). *How Students Learn: Reforming Schools Through Learner-Centered Instruction* (Washington, DC: American Psychological Association, 1998).

Chapter 4

One Teacher, Many Roles

"As a teacher, I have realized that satisfaction comes not by having all the answers, but by watching others find them."

Charles Epps (*Numb3rs*)

Defining Roles

At first glance, the art teacher who uses Differentiated Instruction seems like someone who is a magician, making many amazing things happen in the classroom all at once. This perception often scares teachers away because it seems like a lot of new things to put on one's plate, but actually, most teachers already have several of the skills they need in their teaching repertoire. DI helps you add some new skills, while using those you already have with greater purpose, honing them with intention and practice until they become highly efficient and effective.

Differentiated art classrooms often look complicated to outside observers because students are not always sitting quietly in rows, but instead are involved in active learning. This shift can cause new teachers or other observers to wonder how to juggle it all—keeping the needs of students and the demands of subject matter in check, while creating true communities of art learning. This chapter will explore the multifaceted roles of a differentiated teacher and give examples of how to accomplish each aspect of those roles.

Warm Demander

When I first heard the term "warm demander" in a training session with Carol Ann Tomlinson, I felt like I finally had an accurate way to describe who I was as a teacher in a differentiated classroom. This term beautifully encompasses the idea of pushing students to achieve more than they think possible, while also supporting them and helping them to believe in themselves and their abilities. A warm demander encourages students through words and actions and helps them see what they are capable of accomplishing, even if they are

PERSONAL CONNECTIONS

Balancing Control

As you read, consider the following questions:

1 What are your greatest strengths as a teacher?

2 Who has ownership over the classroom space, supplies, and activities that happen in the space where you teach?

3 Are there aspects of learning that you rush over or omit due to limited class time, even though you know that these experiences would build deeper meaning or connection between students and the topic they are exploring?

unsure of themselves. A warm demander is also not satisfied when students think they already know everything; instead, they expect and encourage these students to reach higher.

As teachers, we know that students live up to the expectations that others have for them. Teachers who expect great things have students who live up to those expectations. Likewise, if little is expected, little will be given. Warm demanders believe that all students can learn and grow with the right kind of support. They expect nothing less than the personal best of each student because they believe in each one. They are not people who yell, scream, or threaten as a means to get what they want; they simply encourage. Warm demanders cheer students on, celebrate their accomplishments, and provide the structure students need to step out into unfamiliar or uncomfortable areas.

When a student gives up because they "can't draw" or they are "not good at art," but you have helped her or him find a way not to give up, you have been a warm demander. Whenever you show students their drawings from the beginning of the year to remind them of how far they have come, you have been a warm demander. Warm demanders help students realize that making art takes time, practice, and patience, and that they will reach their goals if they stick with it.

When my students became discouraged because they couldn't create art like I did, I would ask them, "How long do you think I have been an artist?" Then, "How long have you been an artist?" Once I pointed out the experience and time differences between our years of making art, they would begin to understand that with time they could get there, too. It is easy to become discouraged, but when someone believes in you, it can go a long way toward building confidence.

THINK POINT

The Importance of Language

Words have the power to build up or tear down. If you question this, just think about a time when someone said that they were disappointed in you. Wow, what an impact that small statement probably had! The words we choose have great power to shape, change, or create behaviors.[1] As teachers, the language we use is critical in creating a classroom environment in which students feel safe, respected, valued, appreciated, and interested in learning.[2]

The words you choose are very important and can convey simple but important messages to your students. Think about using words or phrases in your classroom language that share ownership and express value in your students—words that include, not exclude. Change phrases like "my classroom," "my lesson," and "my plan" to things like "our classroom," "our lesson," and "our plan." Create a sense of shared responsibility by using the word *team* when referring to your class or a small group within your class.

These seem like minor changes, but they can quickly reshape students' ideas, actions, and values in positive ways. Inclusive language tells students they are important and gives them a sense of purpose and ownership as valuable participants in something beyond themselves.

Partner in Learning

When I was growing up, my parents wanted me to understand the value of earning the things I wanted, so I had to work hard and save money to pay for some of the special things I wanted to do or own. This accomplished two important goals: it gave me a sense of ownership over what I had worked hard to earn; it gave me pride in what I had accomplished. The items I earned became my own and I treasured them. Similarly, being a partner in learning means that you, as a teacher, leave space for your students to explore and discover knowledge in ways that allow them to work with ideas, sometimes even wrestle with them, so that they have ownership and pride over what they have accomplished.

Your role as a partner in learning means that you listen to your students and value their ideas. It means that you back up a bit and allow space for students to think, make choices, take on leadership roles, and sometimes decide the next direction that they need to take in their learning process. With this perspective, education becomes a partnership in which students learn that they are responsible for their education; they must work hard, seek answers, contribute to a positive classroom environment, and ask questions. They cannot expect to sit around and have everything given to them.

Giving students a voice does not mean that you are not in charge of what they learn and do. You still decide what content the class should cover and how, you have the last word in matters of classroom management, and you are the captain of the ship; however, good leaders know that it is best to win people over by listening, encouraging, and supporting them. You are the master architect who sets up the framework on which students can build as they explore ideas, artworks, and media. You are helping your students to discover knowledge, as opposed to constantly providing them with information; this helps students build ownership in what they are learning. A role model is a partner who places trust and value in students, and empowers them to take charge of their classroom and their learning. This can begin in small ways by having students make classroom decisions, taking charge of certain aspects of a lesson, or even by letting them explore a topic and share their thoughts or ideas.

As students become more independent and realize that they can and are expected to make decisions, and that they don't need to run to you for every answer, you might feel as if you are not as necessary as you once were. Don't be fooled; you are

PERSPECTIVES

"Behold the turtle. He makes progress only when he sticks his neck out."
James Bryant Conant

still needed, but in different ways. After implementing DI in her classroom, a teacher with whom I worked came to me because she was worried that she was "not teaching" anymore. She was no longer lecturing or always standing at the front of the class. She usually found herself going around the room talking with students, offering them encouragement, checking on their progress, and asking questions to encourage them to dig deeper. This was a major shift in her role and it took some time for her to feel comfortable with allowing students to have more control of their learning. She soon realized that she did not have to talk or lecture in the front of the classroom all the time or repeatedly answer the same questions in order to be seen as a teacher. Once she realized that students were demonstrating initiative and learning in deeper ways than before, she embraced the new role that allowed her the freedom to talk with students on an individual basis and strengthen her relationships with them.

Depending on your current classroom situation, you may already think of yourself as a partner in learning with your students, or it may be something completely new that you will want to try in gradual ways. Something as simple as asking students what type of rules they would like to have in their art class opens the door for their voices to be heard. If this is a new area for you and you feel that your students have not shown enough responsibility to entrust them with decisions, then let them make small decisions at first. Explain that you are doing this to show your trust in them and to give them more of a voice in the class.

Placing trust in students is a powerful tool that can encourage them and change not only how you interact with students, but also how they interact with each other. For example, disciplinary issues consistently plagued one group of students in my classroom. I wondered if DI would work in this situation. How could I place my trust in these students? I decided to take a risk and try to earn their trust, thinking that this might help to foster an environment of respect. My first step was to have a class meeting where I laid out my plans. I stated that I had a great idea for a project in which they would get to choose the media and topic, but that I knew it could only work if they were willing to show respect to each other and use the media responsibly. I let the students know that their ideas were essential in making the project work. I asked them to vote on whether they thought they personally could handle this assignment and to raise their hands only if they were 100% certain that they could share their own ideas while being responsible and respectful of others. All but one reluctant student raised their hands and, after a pause, he joined in, too.

I immediately asked them what their favorite things or memories were and told them one of my own memories to get them thinking. As a group, students shared a few of their ideas out loud. Next, I asked each of them, without talking to their classmates, to write down or draw on their own three to five objects or memories that were important to them. Then I had them rank these items in order of importance, circling the item they had ranked number one, as most important. On the title line of a four-room thoughts graphic organizer (see Fig. 4.1), I had them write down their number-one choice and then begin to fill in words or phrases about their object or memory using the four categories: sights/visual, (colors, shapes, textures, etc.), sounds, thoughts, one descriptive word repeated three times. The boxes, or rooms, in the organizer served as repositories for the words they had collected and provided a way for them to recall descriptive details about the topics they had chosen.

Using these collections of words, students wrote song lyrics, short stories, poems, or simple strings of words to use in their mixed-media collages. Because of the personal connections they had with their topics and the freedom to make choices about how their art would look and how they would display it, students demonstrated a significant amount of ownership of their works.

When students got too loud or were distracted, other students would usually make comments to remind them to refocus so they didn't ruin the project for the whole class. Whenever students did not handle the art supplies responsibly, I would remind them that this was their project and that the supplies would only be available if students properly cared for them. My verbal reminder did not garner results on one occasion, so in front of the whole class I asked a very vocal student how she would feel if she couldn't use a certain supply anymore because someone else didn't care for it. She stated that she would be very mad. Then I turned my attention back to the class and asked everyone to pitch in and make sure all the supplies were cared for and put back where they belonged.

This one question made the point that the supplies in the room belong to the students, they are responsible for those supplies, and that it is important to care for them so they will always be available; it also helped to avoid lecturing the class or placing blame on an individual. As partners in learning, teachers help students gain ownership over the classroom space, the supplies, their actions, and their own learning. When this sense of shared ownership occurs in a classroom, students value that space more, as well as everything in it; they have transformed the teacher's classroom into their own classroom.

Name: ______________________

Four-Room Thoughts

Title: ______________________

Sounds	Sights/Visuals
Thoughts	**One descriptive word repeated three times**

Take your words from the boxes above and use them to write a song, short story, or poem. You may also add others words to aid you in the writing, just be sure to use at least five words from the above boxes. Somewhere on the collage of your most important thing you must include at least five words in some format. They could be obvious or hidden within the piece.

____

____

____

____

4.1 *Four-Room Thoughts Graphic Organizer.* Graphic organizers can be powerful tools in aiding students to gather, reflect, and recall information. Created by Heather L. R. Fountain.

4.2 *Lost in the Mountains.* A student used the information from her four-room thoughts graphic organizer to create a collage about a family trip that turned scary. Photo by Heather L. R. Fountain.

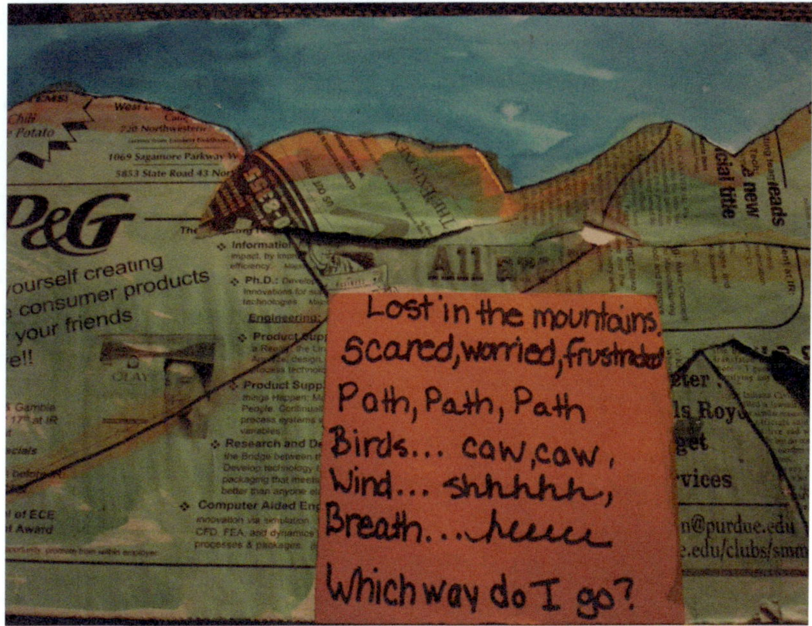

Another important element of this partner-in-learning role is that your students see you as a learner—someone who seeks knowledge. It is important for them to see you not as someone who already has all the answers, but as someone from whom they can learn many lessons as they watch how you learn.

This became apparent to me during my first year of teaching when a student asked me how to spell a word. Anyone who knows me well knows that spelling isn't my strong point. My first thought was, "Oh no! I can't spell. They're going to find out." Teachers are supposed to know everything, right? For some reason, my mouth took over and said, "Hmm…I'm not sure. Let's figure it out." We went over to the dictionary and tried looking up the word, to no avail; then we moved to the computer to spell-check the word. The student sounded out the word, typed it into the computer, and used the spell-check function. Lo and behold the word appeared and it started with the letter *e*, not the letter *a* as we had both assumed.

That day, my student and I learned more than how to spell a word. My student learned strategies to help him figure out how to look up answers when he is unsure. He also learned that it is okay to admit when you don't know something. I learned that, even as a teacher, I don't have to know everything. That small interaction helped me see that it is more important for me to teach my students how to be learners and solve problems than it is to have all of the answers all of the time. They often learn as much from what I *don't* know, which leads us in interesting directions as we seek the answers together as partners in learning.

Proactive Designer

Proactive designers understand the core concept that teachers teach students subjects, not subjects to students. In this way of thinking, students become the first consideration in designing curriculum, rather than an afterthought. Even if you are

MAJOR POINTS

Proactive vs. Reactive Curriculum Design

Proactive curriculum design refers to planning and designing learning experiences and your classroom space with students' needs in mind from the start. How is this different from creating a lesson plan before teaching a lesson, like most teachers already do?

In a traditional lesson plan that is not differentiated, teachers often focus on the content to be taught without considering students' learning needs. In this situation, if students have problems learning, then teachers *react* and try to adapt or modify the lesson to address those problems. This approach is reactive planning.

When you proactively plan, you think of your students' different learning styles and needs before and during your planning, not after they have experienced difficulties. A proactively designed lesson helps students gain knowledge and skills while preserving their dignity as learners. Although you cannot always know every student's learning needs ahead of time, you can proactively consider most of them in your plans; this will reduce the amount of reactive planning you will have to accomplish and the amount of frustration students might experience during class time.

TRY THIS

Students with Limited Fine-Motor Skills

If you have students who have limited fine-motor skills, differentiate your lessons by providing one of the following adaptations:

- Provide special scissors, found in art supply catalogues, that make cutting easier.
- Allow students to rip or tear items instead of cutting them with scissors.
- With a razor-blade or knife, make a small slit on the top and on the bottom of an old racquet ball and slide the handle of a paintbrush through the slits; this will allow the student to hold the larger, modified handle.
- Buy paintbrushes that have egg-shaped handles.
- Place a ball of white, foamlike, self-hardening clay around the handle of a pencil, marker, or paintbrush and have the student immediately grip the clay in a way that feels comfortable. The clay will harden in the shape of the student's grip, but will be pliable enough to remove when necessary.
- Provide a larger paper or canvas space on which the student will work. This will allow her or him to make larger, easier movements with the hands.

expected to use a required curriculum guide or schedule, you still are the one who decides *how* to teach your students the curriculum content and what environment you will create to foster their learning; this is a proactive approach.

The key difference between designing a lesson plan and being a proactive designer of lessons is that you use the knowledge that you have gathered about your students, in conjunction with your knowledge of the topic, to design an enriching learning experience for all students. In some cases, the knowledge about your students is very specific, such as a learning disability or a fear or particular interest, while in other cases, your knowledge is more abstract and draws from learning styles and multiple intelligences theories.

I had a student who, due to physical disabilities, had difficulty using scissors and glue bottles. When proactively planning for a collage project, I included in my lesson the option for students to use scissors or to rip paper with their hands. I also had a special box of precut images, fabric swatches, and other collage items from which students could choose up to three options to use in their work. Additionally, students had the choice of using glue bottles, glue sticks of various sizes, or glue in portion cups. This simple, proactive design helped vary the way students could incorporate diverse items into their collages, and it also ensured that they could successfully use the materials without struggling, and that no one would be excluded.

THEORIES AND TERMS

Flexibly Managing Your Classroom

There are many aspects of classroom management that teachers juggle every day. The careful and flexible management of the following elements of the classroom environment can help to differentiate instruction in valuable ways:

- **Grouping** Consider the use of small groups, interest-based groups, or pair partners.
- **Pacing** Consider what options to provide for students who finish early or who need more time to complete tasks.
- **Materials** Consider whether the whole class will work with the same materials, and if not, how you will introduce different materials.
- **Noise** Consider whether activities should be loud, quiet, or silent.
- **Support** Consider what level of support to provide students, from those who need their own space to those who need consistent encouragement.
- **Timing** Consider how you will use timing in your class. Will there be one long work time, smaller chunks of work time with varied activities, or a demonstration break in the middle of a class period?
- **Content** Consider how content could evolve from what you had planned to what arises during class, such as tangents, student-led questions, or class discoveries.
- **Assessment** Consider how much, how often, and what type of assessment will provide the information you need. Also consider the timing of your assessment; when is the best time to assess?
- **Communication** Consider which type of communication—verbal, written, or visual—matches the needs of your students and the goals of the lesson you have planned.

Flexible Manager

Flexibility is one of the keys to meeting students' needs. Teachers who are flexible managers understand that learning in the classroom often will not look or play out the same way every day, but will change with the needs of the learners. Flexible teachers are often described as those who can think on their feet. They look around and assess a situation in the blink of an eye, and if changes need to occur, they make them happen fairly seamlessly. They also allow students to question and bring forward ideas, knowledge, and experiences that could lead in different directions than those initially planned. Taking advantage of these moments can lead to golden opportunities for learning that build on the original lesson plan in ways that the teacher had not considered.

Time is often the most difficult area to manage flexibly. As art teachers, we often worry about the limited amount of time that we have with students and we want to get in as much content as possible when we see them. It took me a

TRY THIS

Graphic Organizers

Have students use a graphic organizer to brainstorm ideas before moving on to the production phase of a project.

Graphic organizers have been shown to help students create deeper meaning in their work, use time more efficiently, and make greater connections to what they are learning. If you are hesitant to give up art time to have students complete a graphic organizer, think about how many times students have said that they don't know what to do or that they have no ideas. Brainstorming eliminates these two problems and gives students many ideas to draw from as they create their artwork. The use of graphic organizers not only meets language arts standards, but it also becomes an advocacy point because you are integrating writing across your curriculum.

★ Our Identity ★

What are some things that make you different from everyone else?	What are some things that are special to you?
+ Personality +	+ My shoes +
What hobbies do you like to do?	**Who influences you in your life?**
+ Play sports + Play guitar +	+ Mr. Cunningham + Dad + Mom

4.3 *Our Identity Graphic Organizer.* Identity is a topic that relates to all people, but is not always something that we take time to think about in depth. A graphic organizer helps to create a specific focus on this topic.
Created by Heather L. R. Fountain.

while to realize that by rushing to get to the project without making connections first wasted more time than if I had provided students with the opportunity to brainstorm or make connections with the topic first. My inflexibility stifled my students' creativity and limited their ability to wonder or dig deeper into learning. It also wasted class time because they were sitting around saying, "I don't know what to do; I have no ideas." When I used time flexibly to help students make connections, they actually used their time more efficiently because they had ideas and were working hard to accomplish their goals. It is not always easy to be flexible, but the careful management of a classroom can lead to incredible connections and discoveries for students and teachers.

TRY THIS

Self-Portrait: What Makes Me Who I Am?

Shake up the average self-portrait project by asking students to compose their portraits out of items that represent who they are and what they are interested in. First, provide them with the think sheet, "What makes me who I am?" Have them fill out as much information as they can about the places and people that are important to them, interests they have, activities they are involved in, and any other items they might want to include. You can differentiate this graphic organizer by providing it in another language or by asking students to draw their answers in each category. Have students use the information from their personal graphic organizers to construct their self-portraits within their own silhouettes.

Other Connections:

- silhouettes
- overlapping
- color mixing
- tints and shades
- artist Giuseppe Arcimboldo

How Is This Differentiated?

This lesson is differentiated because it allows students to draw from their own personal interests to create self-portraits. You can also differentiate it through the use of varied instructions on the think sheet, by allowing students to draw their answers, or by providing the sheet in a language more familiar to your students.

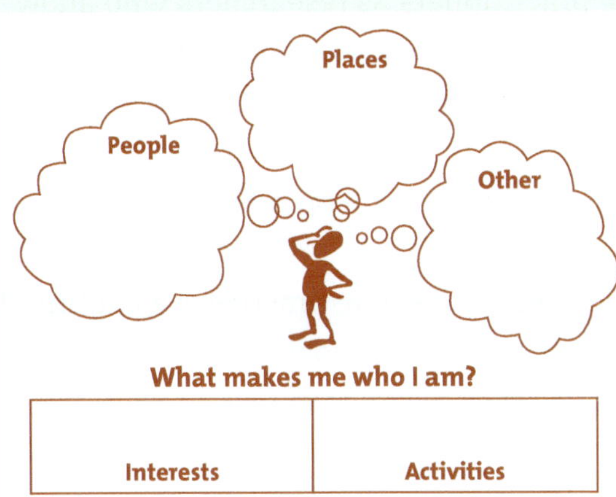

4.4 *Think Sheet—What Makes Me Who I Am?* **Students often have difficulty coming up with ideas when they start a new art project. A think sheet used for brainstorming guides students in reflection, helping them find direction as they develop their ideas.** Created by Heather L. R. Fountain.

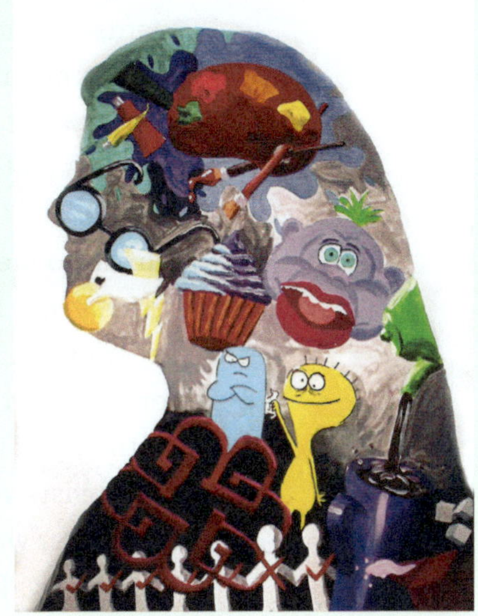

4.5 *What Makes Me Who I Am?* self-portrait painting. Photo by Rachele Trzcinski.

PERSPECTIVES

"Follow effective action with quiet reflection. From the quiet reflection will come even more effective action." Peter Drucker, Educator and Writer

Reflective Practitioner

As art teachers, we often are busy teaching multiple classes or even hundreds of students a day, so the thought of taking time to reflect seems like a luxury. This type of reflection-in-action can happen over time or even in a moment, such as when problems occur and need immediate attention. Each moment of reflection allows teachers to consider thoughtfully how their actions affect their students, while building a repertoire or collection of ideas, experiences, images, examples, and actions that they can drawn upon in the future when problems arise.

The concept of a reflective practitioner is not a new one, nor is it specific to Differentiated Instruction, yet it is one of the most important roles played by teachers. In 1983, Donald Schön described reflective practitioners as researchers who allow themselves to experience surprise, wonder, and even confusion in unfamiliar situations.[3] They then use reflection and their prior knowledge as they carry out experiments to help them understand the situation and decide on new actions.

Similar to lifelong learning, reflective practice is a continual process that helps professionals to grow and learn from their experiences. Reflective practice can take many forms, from conversation and writings to the creation of artwork. Which method you use for reflection is not important; the method that assists you in reflecting on your teaching practice in a way that works best with your learning style is. In their *Translations: Teaching Art as Reflective Craft*, Kathy Unrath and Carrie Nordlund point out that reflective practitioners "collect data, analyze actions, and most importantly develop solutions to real teaching problems and limitations."[4] Just remember that although reflection is not always comfortable for you, as it makes you examine yourself and your teaching practices, it will lead you to stretch and grow in positive ways that will benefit both you and your students.

Conclusion

PERSPECTIVES

"Be not afraid of going slowly; be afraid only of standing still." Chinese Proverb

As teachers, we do the best we can with what we have each day. Some days are easier than others, and some will leave us scratching our heads wondering what went wrong. Teachers who use DI are not perfect, but seek to grow and learn along with their students. You may already see elements of yourself in many of the teacher roles that we have considered in this chapter, as I did when I first began. Just remember that these roles ask you to do what you expect your students to do: Believe in yourself enough to take steps forward, growing along the way.

REFLECTION & PRACTICE

Balancing Control

1 **Teacher Role** In what ways are you a magician who makes amazing things happen in your classroom? Sometimes we are so close to what we do every day that we can't see it clearly. If that is the case for you, ask a colleague to observe you and take note of the magical things you help students do. Another way to gauge this is to ask students to fill out an anonymous exit card listing their favorite thing about you as their teacher and one thing they would like you to do more of.

2 **Student Voice** Think of one way that you can help students feel comfortable expressing their ideas about their learning this week. This could be a time when they can express their opinions and ideas about their next project, the current topic being explored in class, or even their constructive criticism about work in progress.

3 **Reflective Practice** For one week, write down what you have done well today and one point for improvement. Let each day's reflection lead you to greater success the next day. At the end of the week, congratulate yourself on the things that you were successful at, and be sure to look at the points for improvement to see if there is a pattern or reoccurring area that needs more work. Ask colleagues or use the Internet to find resources and information about that topic to help you improve in that area.

Notes

1 L. S. Vygotsky, *Thought and Language* (Cambridge, MA: MIT Press, 1986).

2 P. Denton, *The Power of Our Words: Teacher Language That Helps Children Learn* (Turners Falls, MA: Northeast Foundation for Children, 2007).

3 D. Schön, (1983). *The Reflective Practitioner: How Professionals Think in Action* (New York: Basic Books, 1983); M. K. Smith, "Donald Schön: Learning, Reflection and Change," *The Encyclopedia of Informal Education*, 2001, www.infed.org/thinkers/et-schon.htm (accessed June 2009).

4 K. Unrath and C. Nordlund, *Translations: Teaching Art as Reflective Craft* (Reston, VA: The National Art Education Association, 2006): p. 3.

Chapter 5

Getting Started

"[When differentiating instruction,] teachers proactively plan varied approaches to what students need to learn, how *they will learn it, and/or* how they will show what they have learned *in order to increase the likelihood that each student will learn as much as he or she can, as efficiently as possible."*

Carol Ann Tomlinson

PERSONAL CONNECTIONS

Gathering Data

As you read, consider the following questions:

1 How do you feel about assessment (positive or negative) and why?

2 In what ways do you already pre-assess your students for readiness, prior knowledge, interests, background, learning styles, and multiple intelligences strengths? If you do not, what has kept you from doing so?

3 What positive aspects of proactive design will help you strengthen your ability to design instruction that engages students in learning about art?

You have become familiar with the idea of what a proactive designer is in chapter four; now it is time to take action. You will need to consider students' interests, learning styles, background experiences, strengths and weaknesses, readiness for learning, disabilities, and even gender-based issues that might affect how they learn. In an art classroom where teachers often see hundreds of students, this may seem like an impossible task, but this chapter will provide some quick, easy ways to gather information you need to begin proactive lesson design.

Proactive Curriculum Design Concepts

By assuming an active role in designing curriculum, we can create experiences that anticipate rather than react to students' learning needs. We can take information gained through pre-assessment or prior experience with students to design a curriculum that draws them in, builds their confidence, and creates a fulfilling learning experience.

At first, you may think that you don't have the time to pre-assess your students. You may see them every week or every day, but most likely you only see them for a short amount of time and you want to take advantage of every minute you have with them. This is understandable; I felt the same way until I realized that not only did pre-assessment not have to be a long, involved process, but it also positively impacted the amount and quality of the class time I had with my students. Pre-assessment garnered many benefits for myself and my students already described in chapter three: student investment increased, more content was covered, and student

MAJOR POINTS

Pre-assessment is the foundation for differentiated lessons.

Pre-assessment will help you gauge:

- What students already know or have learned about a topic, enabling you to skip content they are familiar with or scaffold topics they have forgotten or have not learned.
- How your students can best learn and connect with knowledge, allowing you to design lessons with varied modes of interaction and content delivery.
- What students' art or general interests are, which you can use to engage your students.

MAJOR POINTS

Pre-assessment

Pre-assessment shows your students that you care about what they know, what they want to know, and what they have already experienced in their lives.

confidence was enhanced. I learned to love pre-assessment. I was a student who hated testing; therefore, even as an adult, I associated assessment with testing, anxiety, and judgment. As I began to increase my use of pre-assessment, my view changed and I discovered that assessment had more to do with helping students grow than with cataloging their mistakes.

The benefits gained by pre-assessment outweighed any initial time it took to achieve them. By the end of the first school year, I noticed that I had covered three more lessons than the year before and had far fewer issues of student discipline. There are a multitude of ways to pre-assess students' readiness, prior knowledge, interests, background, learning styles, and multiple intelligences strengths. Choosing which option will meet your needs depends on what you want to know.

Using Students' Interests and Background

"If students are interested in what they're doing they won't need to come up with distractions or find something they'd rather be doing." Dennis Littky[1]

Since students' interests and background are important in fostering motivation and connection to learning, as well as building relationships, it is recommended that you start this type of pre-assessment right away, if not the first day of class. With pre-assessment, you will immediately express to your students that you care about their interests and ideas, and this is the first step in showing your students that they are important. The inventory of interests, hobbies, important concerns, likes, dislikes, and so on will also build a list of ideas to help your students when they get stuck. When you hear the infamous, "I don't know what to do," you can encourage students to choose a topic from their interest inventory. Quite often, this solves the problem and helps them make a choice quickly, or at least it provides some options where they thought there were none.

I once observed a pre-service teacher who adeptly used the background knowledge of her students to hook them into a lesson. She knew that a majority of her students had recently moved from other countries. Many students continually included the themes of family and the countries they had moved from into their artwork. With this in mind, she designed a lesson around memories of special places and shared with them images of the work of artist Do-Ho Suh. They immediately connected to his idea of taking your home with you wherever you go as they viewed his silken home sculptures that he could pack up and move with him wherever he went.

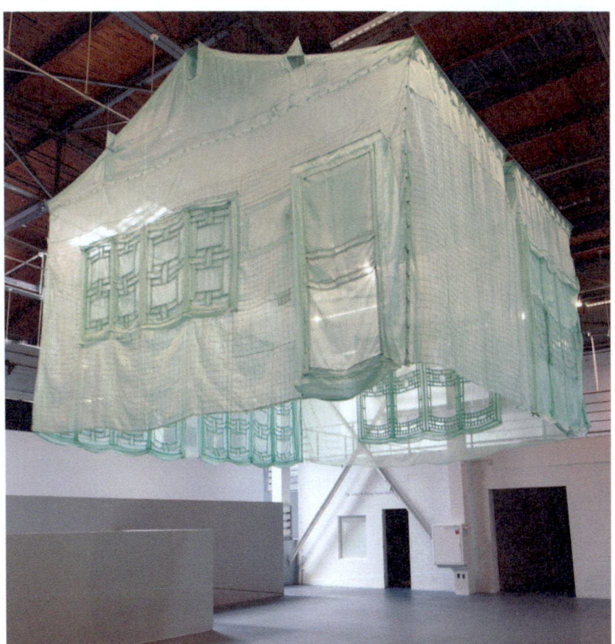

5.1 Do-Ho Suh, *Seoul Home/ L.A. Home*, Silk, 1999.

Examples of Students' General Interests Pre-Assessment

A common way to gather pre-assessment information about students is to have them fill out a questionnaire or sheet with the answers to your questions. Although that can work, I have included an art activity as part of the process of gathering information in the examples shown, which will give you more information to work with, and the process is more enjoyable. Each pre-assessment tool has its own specific purpose, directions, and an example. Several of them gather more information than basic interests or, at least, leave the door open for students to add important things they would like you to know in confidence. This open-door option has lead to students sharing issues such as sexual identity, their choice to be a vegan, or their fears as a result of a learning disability.

PRE-ASSESSMENT TOOL

People Puzzle

Purpose

To assess student interests, styles, and level of art skills, while emphasizing the concept of unity and how, while each of us has our own different abilities and interests, together we make an interesting and complete team.

Teacher Directions

You can modify this idea to create a class puzzle or a whole-school puzzle. You could even turn this into a school mural or tile mosaic to display in your school's lobby.

1. To create a basic puzzle shape, draw four lines horizontally on a piece of white drawing paper to create equal-sized sections.
2. Draw a variety of curved and angled lines in each horizontal section to create odd shapes. You should have a total number of shapes to equal the number of students in the class. Be sure to number each piece lightly in pencil to assist students in putting the puzzle back together.
3. Cut out the pieces and place them on a table for students to choose.

continued on next page

Student Directions

1 Choose one piece of the puzzle and write your name, interests, favorite things, and anything else you think is important for me to know on the side without a number. This side of the puzzle piece will be kept confidential and will only be seen by you and me.

2 On the other side of your piece, design your name or initials in a way that expresses your style.

3 When you have a completed your puzzle piece, bring it to the front table and place it where it belongs to complete the puzzle.

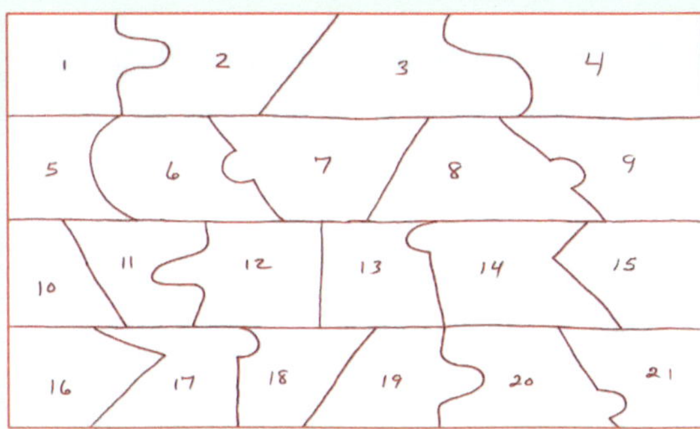

5.2 *People Puzzle Blank Example.* You can quickly turn a simple piece of white paper into a puzzle. Created by Heather L. R. Fountain.

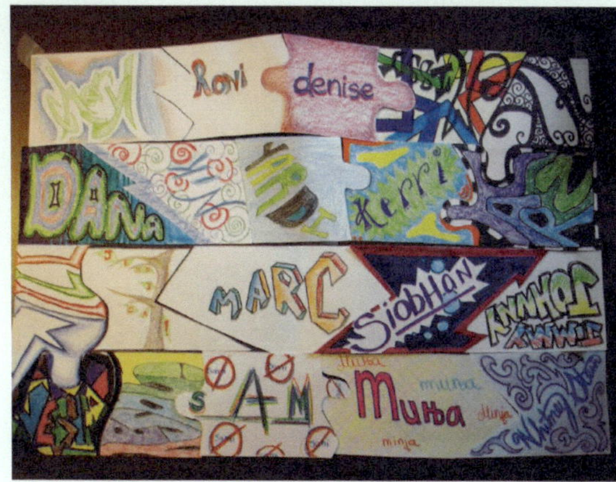

5.3 *Completed People Puzzle.* Individual puzzle pieces come together to create a visual metaphor representing how different people come together to create a beautiful, well-rounded whole. Photo by Heather L. R. Fountain.

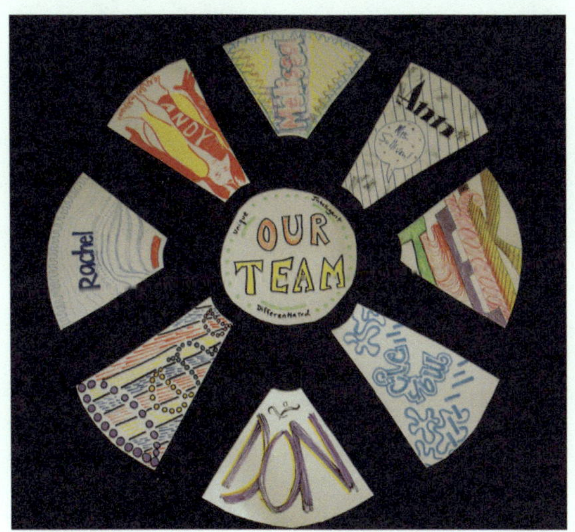

5.4 *Class Mosaic Puzzle.* By modifying the People Puzzle, you can create the Mosaic Puzzle on paper or tiles and install it in your school. Photo by Heather L. R. Fountain.

PRE-ASSESSMENT TOOL

Expressive Group Puzzle

This is a variation of the People Puzzle. It works well for table teams or small groups.

Purpose

To assess student interests, styles, and levels of art skills, while emphasizing the concept of unity and how, while each of us has our own different skills and interests, together we make an interesting and complete team.

Teacher Directions

Provide one piece of drawing paper to each group and various drawing media.

Student Directions

1 As a team, decide on a shape that best represents your group.

2 Using paper, cut out your shape, just one, as large as you can.

3 Cut the shape into pieces like a puzzle. The number of pieces should equal the number of group members.

4 On the front side of your puzzle piece, design your name in a typestyle and colors that best define your personality. Be sure to think about how you can use line, shape, and color in expressive ways.

5 On the back side of your puzzle piece write down all the things that are important to you. Include at least two hobbies and two things you would like to do in art class this year.

6 You can add anything to your puzzle piece that you want me to know. The back will be seen by only you and me.

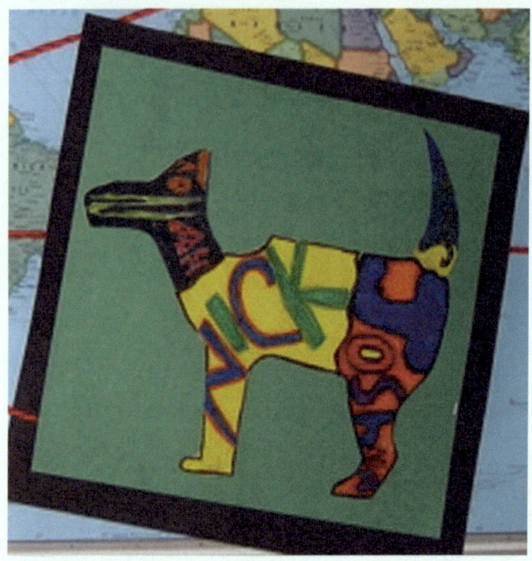

5.5 *Expressive Group Puzzle*. Created by middle school students, this variation of the People Puzzle places the decision of puzzle shape in the hands of the group members. It also requires members of the group to discuss, negotiate, and work together to accomplish their final puzzle. Photo by Kristen Tuerk.

PRE-ASSESSMENT TOOL

Personal Identity Museum

Purpose

To assess student interests while teaching them about the job of a museum curator and about the use of art elements and principles to express their ideas through the arrangement and display of objects.

Teacher Directions

Provide each student in your class with one small bag to fill with items and one copy of the *Museum Guide Sheet* (A.5.1).

Student Directions

Day 1 Take home your brown-paper bag and fill it with objects that express who you are and things that are important to you. You may have no more than one photograph in your collection. You will only be able to use the items that are in your bag to create your personal identity museum.

Day 2 You have ten to twelve minutes to find a location in the room and set up your museum. As curator, please fill out the Museum Guide Sheet to assist the patrons in interpreting your collection.

Day 3 Place your Museum Guide Sheet in a location near your collection. Be sure it does not detract from your museum display.

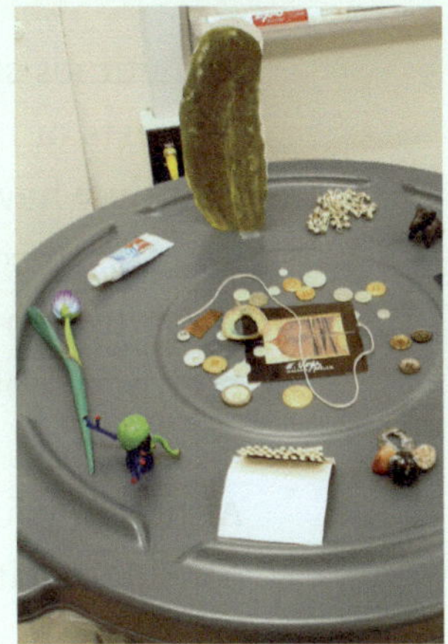

5.6 Get to know your students through the items they choose to share in their personal museums. Photo by Heather L. R. Fountain.

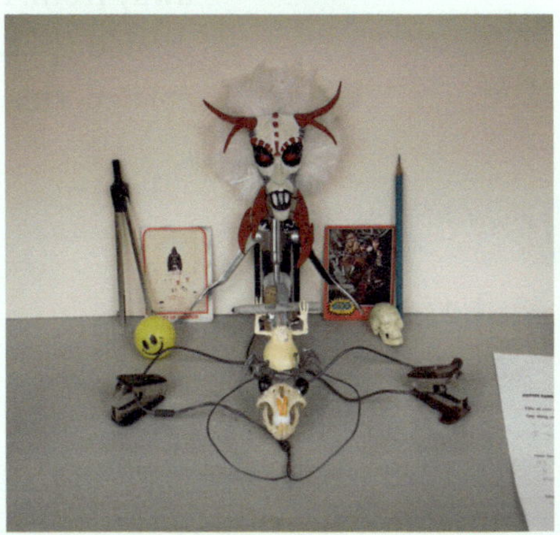

5.7 Students become the curators of their own museum and decide what items they will include in their collections, and how they will display these items for viewing. Photo by Heather L. R. Fountain.

Examples of Students' Art Interests Pre-Assessment

Sometimes students will not include art topics on their general interests or hobbies list, but that does not necessarily mean that they have no preference as to what they want to learn in art class. It could simply mean that they have not figured out what does interest them in art, as there are so many things they have not experienced or learned about yet.

Although you will design lessons around topics they have not considered, it is helpful to know what media, ideas, and topics students are most excited about and what topics they shy away from. Pre-assessment will give you a quick list of art ideas related to students' interests that you can use when designing curriculum.

PRE-ASSESSMENT TOOL

What Makes Me ME

Purpose

To assess students' interests and motor-skill abilities in a fun and creative way that helps them think about how line, shape, and color can reflect personality traits.

Teacher Directions

Provide one copy of the *What Makes Me ME* sheet (A.5.2 in Appendix) to each student.

Student Directions

1 Read the directions on the What Makes Me ME sheet.

2 Fill in all the information to the best of your ability.

3 Draw a vessel such as a vase, bowl, or other container in a shape you like best. Will it be big or small? Will it have handles? Will it have curved or straight lines?

4 Add designs, patterns, lines, and colors to your vessel to show what things you like and to express your personality.

5 Please put your name on the back of your vessel.

PRE-ASSESSMENT TOOL

In Art I Hope We...Pie Chart

Purpose
To assess students' art interests in a visual way, while showing how visual thinking skills apply to other subjects such as math.

Student Directions

1 Decide what things you would most like to do in art this year.

2 Using a percentage, write down how excited you are to do each item. Be sure your numbers add up to 100%.

3 Using a paper circle, create a color pie chart with labels that show the things you are most excited about.

4 When you are done coloring and labeling your sections, be sure to add your name on the front of the chart.

5 On the back of your pie chart, tell me about you; add anything about yourself that you would like me to know. Be sure to include your interests, hobbies, and anything else you like. Only you and I will see the back of the chart.

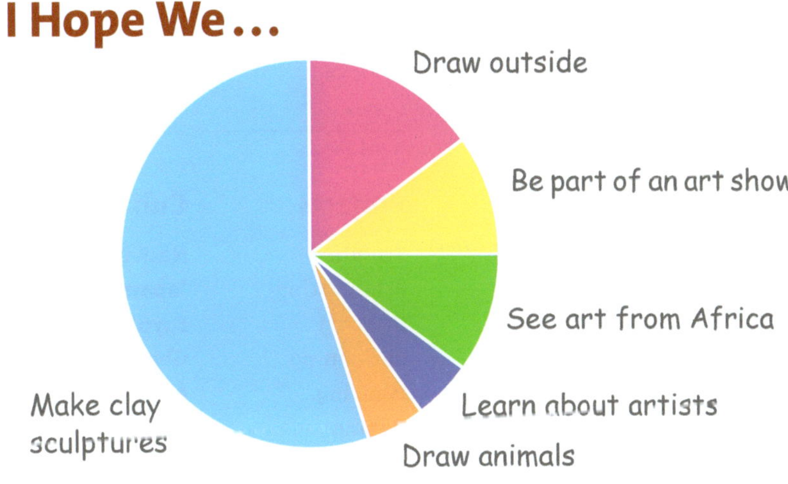

5.8 Pie charts are a quick ways to identify students' interests.
Designed by Carrie Miller.

PRE-ASSESSMENT TOOL

Palette of Choices

Purpose
To assess students' art interests in a visual way, while introducing them to options they may not have considered on their own.

Teacher Directions
Create a list of ideas, media, artists, projects, and cultures that you would like to teach your students during the course of the year.

Student Directions

1 Look at the options and decide what things you would like to do most in art this year.

2 In each category, circle three choices.

3 If there is another option or maybe two that you just can't live without, you may also circle those.

4 Place a star next to your overall top three to five choices.

5 Write your name and class on your sheet.

6 On the back of your sheet, describe any other art topic ideas that you would like to share with me.

This Year in Art I Hope We Learn About...

Name and class: ______________________________

Media	Artists	Big Ideas	Projects	Cultures
Clay	Lydia Corbett	Connecting with Nature	Sculpture	Native American
Paint	Andy Warhol	Imaginary Worlds	Printmaking	Japanese
Charcoal	Vincent van Gogh	Communities in Celebration	Drawing	Egyptian
Yarn	Faith Ringgold	Creative Careers	Cartooning	Ghanaian
Pastels	Alice Neel	Responding to the Arts	Weaving	Mexican
Photography	Sandy Skoglund		Sewing	Australian
Digital Media	Dale Chihuly		Animation	Inuit/Alaskan
Recycled Materials	Piet Mondrian		Collage	Prehistoric
	Horace Pippin		Graphic Design	

5.9 Help students feel a sense of ownership on the first day of class by giving them a chance to make choices and express their interests. Created by Bette Naughton.

PRE-ASSESSMENT TOOL

My Paint Palette—Students with Limited Fine Motor Skills

Purpose

To assess student art topic interests in a way that is accessible for students with limited motor skills or writing ability, while providing an opportunity to strengthen their hands by cutting and pasting.

Teacher Directions

Create and then photocopy your own version of the "This Year in Art I Hope We Learn About..." worksheet (Fig. 5.10) and one sheet with an image of a paint palette for each of the students in your class.

Student Directions

1 Look at the images and words on your This Year in Art I Hope We Learn About... worksheet

2 Decide what things you would most like to learn about in art this year.

3 Cut out the words and pictures of those things and glue them onto your paint palette.

4 Write your name on your paint palette using any colors you want.

5 Add decorative elements and any other words or pictures of things you hope to learn about in art this year.

Name______________________________

This Year in Art I Hope We Learn About....

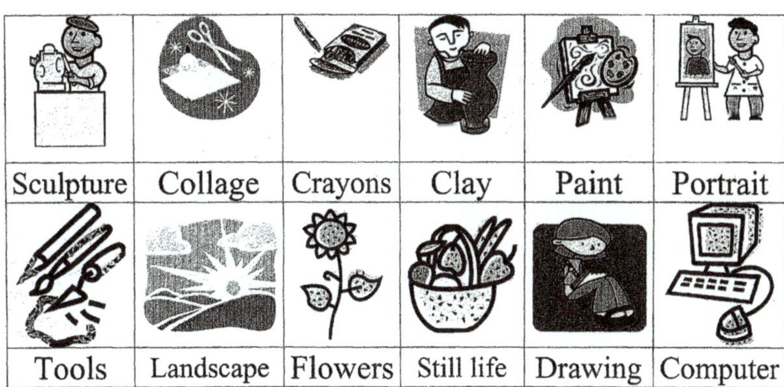

5.10 This pre-assessment tool provides the teacher with an opportunity to assess students' abilities to cut, glue, and make choices. Created by Bette Naughton.

Although knowledge of your students' backgrounds and interests can help you design curriculum and options that help them invest and connect to learning, it can also help you build personal connections with your students. Robyn Jackson talks about the concept of currency in the classroom. She believes that knowing about your students and what they value tells you what their currency is and can even reveal the language of their hearts.[2] I was able to capitalize on this concept when dealing with a young man who had been repeatedly disruptive in class one day. I had him come back later that day to meet with me and discuss his behavior. Unsure what the cause was, I hoped to find out what was going on.

Before meeting with the student, I looked at his "interest" puzzle piece (we had previously worked on a class mosaic puzzle which you can find on p. 89) and noticed that like me, he loves hockey. I used this connection to develop a contract and used sports as the language to connect with him. I asked him questions to help him think about what a contract means in hockey, what responsibilities and consequences are included in the contract, and what happens when a player breaks his contract.

After our talk, I created an art contract that used sports language, and had him fill in three consequences at the bottom of the page that would only be used if he broke his contract. Both he and I agreed on the terms of the contract and he signed on the "art team player" line and I signed on the "art coach" line. From that day onwards, through the four years that I had this student in class, his behavior changed and he became a contributing member of the class and even a leader. The art contract stayed in my drawer and I never brought it out again, but it represented an important lesson for me about the power of knowing my students.

Using Students' Prior Knowledge and Readiness

As you can see, there are many ways to pre-assess your students' prior knowledge and readiness, so you'll want to decide what exactly you want to know in order to choose a pre-assessment strategy.

If you want to know what your class as a whole knows about a topic in general, you could use a simple strategy such as a KWL chart and brainstorm as a class what students already *Know* and what they *Want to Know* about the topic.[3] At the end of the lesson or as it progresses, students can fill out the last column with the things they have *Learned.*

A teacher can use this method with any topic and it quickly reveals what the class knows about the subject while refreshing memories or introducing new ideas as peers contribute to the chart. This method does not help you gain an idea of what individual students know, and does not take into account the ideas of quiet or shy students who might not respond in a whole-group situation. If you want to gather information that will provide a more detailed look at what students know, here are a few modifications to this idea:

1 Have students fill out the KWL chart in small groups.

2 Have individual students complete their own KWL.

3 Ask students by group or table to add to the chart throughout the class period as they work on other things.

5.11 *KWL Civil Rights*. KWL charts help students recall and reflect on what they know and have learned. This visual technique for gathering information shows students their learning progress. Created by Heather L. R. Fountain.

Civil Rights

Know	Want to Know	Learned

PRE-ASSESSMENT TOOL

Checklists

Create checklists to pre-assess what information students already know about using a specific medium. This will help you quickly gauge what students have learned, what techniques you might need to revisit, and what techniques are completely new.

Self-created scales such as figure 5.13 on p. 99, checklists, or inventories can also help you gather specific information about what students know. One such inventory is the "Ladder of Knowledge." Like the KWL, you can use this tool to pre-assess any subject. Students are asked to write the things they know about a topic on each rung of the ladder, starting at the bottom. The intention is that they will brainstorm and try to recall what they know, but as they learn more they will also add to the ladder to show their knowledge growth.

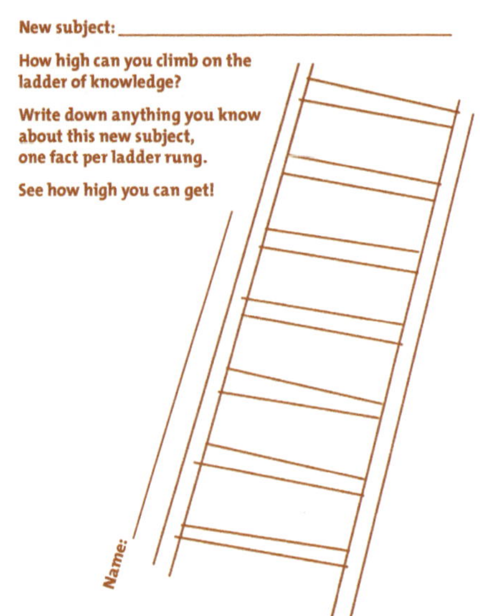

5.12 *Ladder of Knowledge Example*. Whether you work with younger or older students, the Ladder of Knowledge will help them see how far they have climbed up the ladder of learning on a chosen topic. Adjust the language on the worksheet to suit the level of students you are working with. Created by Stacie Kutz.

5.13 *Watercolor Rating Scale Example.* When you use a rating scale, you don't have to wonder what students know. This tool will also allow you to shape your lessons to meet your students' needs. Created by Heather L. R. Fountain.

Watercolor Rating

1. I've never heard of this before.
2. I've heard of this, but am not sure how it works.
3. I know about this and how to use it.

______ Salting
______ Wet on Wet
______ Dry Brush
______ Masking
______ Sgraffito
______ Wash
______ Lifting Out

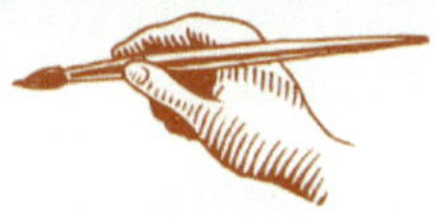

Another useful pre-assessment tool is to have students fill out a "Visual Thinking Map." They have been found to increase listening skills, because students want to have the correct and complete information on their charts.

How to create a Visual Thinking Map:

1 Draw an oval in the center of a page; place the title of the topic that you want students to consider in the oval.

2 Around the topic, place words that relate to ideas, facts, or other pertinent information on which you would like students to reflect.

3 Students can circle any word that relates to something they know and draw a line from that word to the main topic or to another word on the page that connects to the original word.

4 Students then write on the line what connection they have made or what fact they know.

VISUAL THINKING STRATEGY

Visual Thinking Map

Student-created maps have been found to:

- Trigger students' memories when they see the related words on the page.
- Provide a visual means for students to make connections with the topic and between the related categories.
- Provide a quick way for students and teachers to see where gaps in learning exist.
- Lead to greater levels of student attention because they want to know if their connections are correct, and they want to fill in anything that is missing from their page.
- Help students with verbal/linguistic and visual/spatial learning styles to think through ideas.
- Provide a visual thinking strategy for students on the autism spectrum.

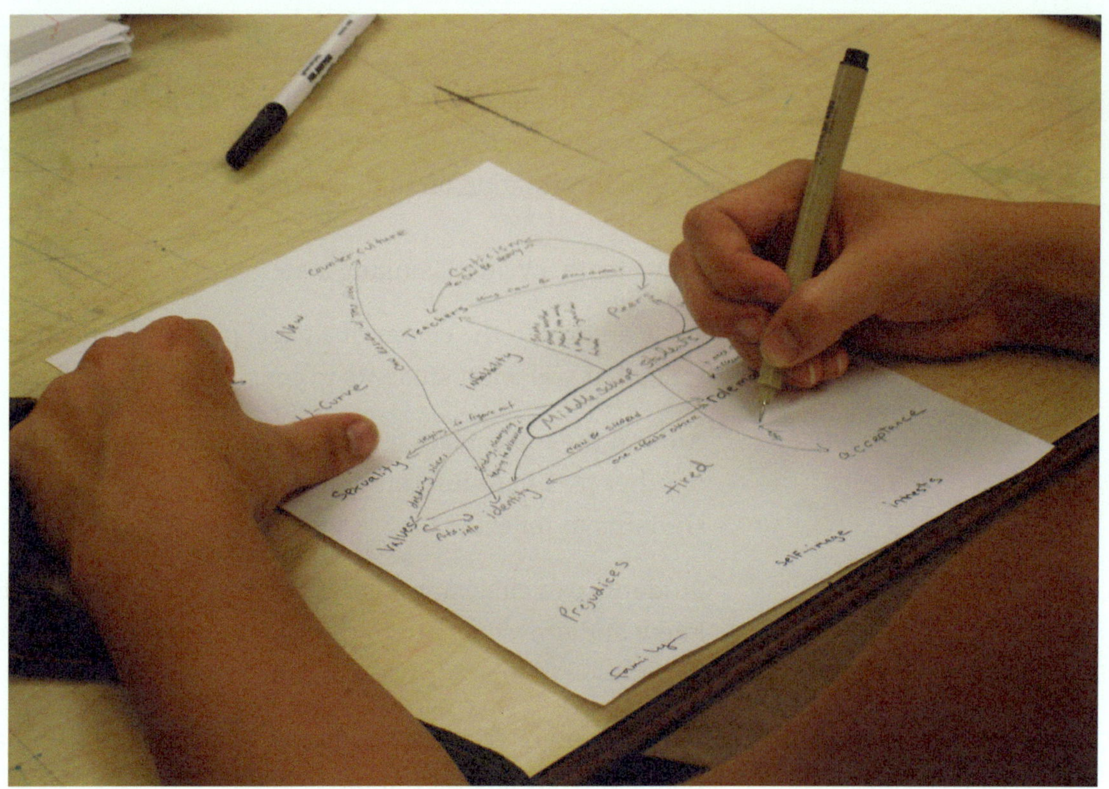

5.14 *Visual Thinking Map Student Example.* Photo by Heather L. R. Fountain.

VISUAL THINKING STRATEGY

Frayer Diagram

For a more complex pre-assessment, you can use a "Frayer Diagram" to assess students' depth of knowledge.[4] The Frayer Diagram consists of four boxes that surround a center word. The topics of the four boxes are: Definition, Key Vocabulary or Characteristics, Examples, and Non-examples. Students consider each box and fill in as much information as they can that relates to the center word.

This graphic organizer was originally created by Dorothy Frayer as a way for students to express their understanding of new words they had learned. In the example provided, I have expanded this format to consider a topic.

This model requires students to use higher order thinking to recall and describe examples and non-examples of the word or topic.

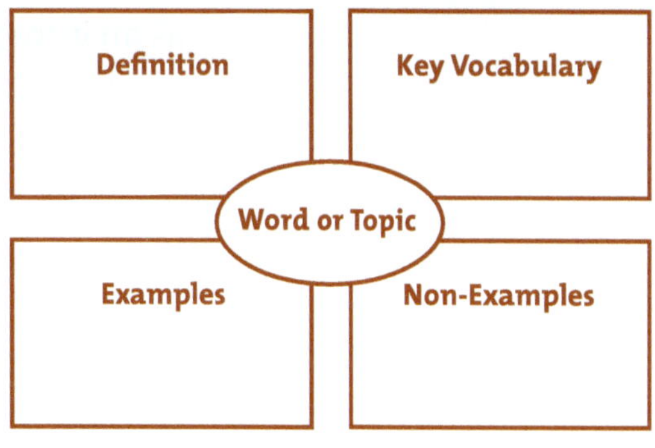

5.15 Blank Frayer Diagram.

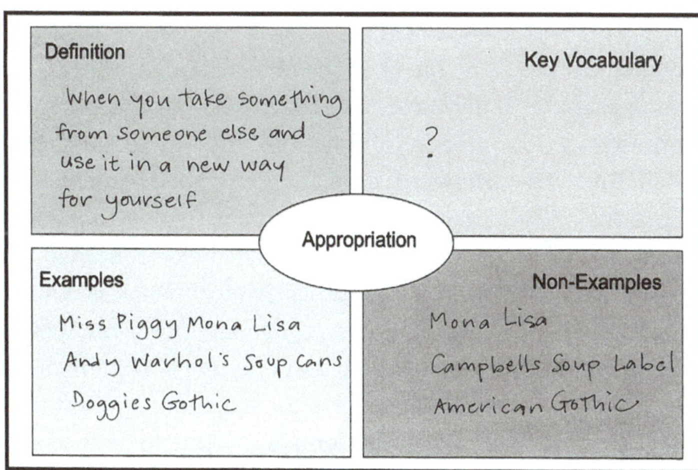

5.16 A Frayer Diagram requires higher-order thinking by asking students not only to write what something is, but also to write what it is not. Created by Heather L. R. Fountain.

You can quickly assess students' abilities such as motor skills or writing levels through an initial art activity that involves one or more skills such as cutting, drawing, gluing, and writing. If you are using an art activity as a pre-assessment, you can use the activity as a jumping-off point for other lessons. For example, you can use the *Exquisite Corpse* exercise on its own as a quick pre-assessment to gauge students' drawing levels, as an introduction to surrealism, or as a way to discuss the benefits and challenges of collaboration before moving on to a larger collaborative project.

You could save enough time at the end of class to have a quick gallery walk so that everyone in the class can see the various combinations that the teams have created. This could lead to a critique session describing what aspects of the drawings students like and why. This critique could also lend itself to a discussion of how to carry the ideas started on the drawings into finished pieces of art.

TRY THIS

Exquisite Corpse Drawings

Briefly introduce students to the surrealist movement and the parlor game the Surrealists invented called "Exquisite Corpse." Form teams comprised of three to five students each. Give team members pieces of paper that have the same dimensions and that they can fold horizontally into equal sections, the same number of sections as the number of members on the team (five team members = five equal horizontal sections on the paper).

Students begin in the top section of the paper, drawing the top or the head of something that they imagine. This could be a self-portrait, the top of an ice cream sundae, or even a mythical creature. After a pre-determined amount of time, ask students to fold over their drawings so that only the bottom inch of the image is visible before they pass them on to another teammate. The next team member will draw a middle section for the image and when time is up, he or she will once again fold the paper over so that only the bottom inch is revealed and pass the paper on. The last transfer provides students with time to draw a bottom or foot section for the image. If there are four or five students per team, have them continue

continued on next page

to pass the paper along until all of the sections are filled. Upon completion, the original artist receives the image back and opens it to reveal the completed creation.

What is differentiated?

The product is differentiated through choice. The students select the topics they draw, their group members, the style they use, and the media.

Why is it differentiated?

This lesson is differentiated to give students more freedom and choice. It is also differentiated in a way that helps students think creatively on their own and use their current ideas, strengths, and levels of ability to accomplish the task at hand.

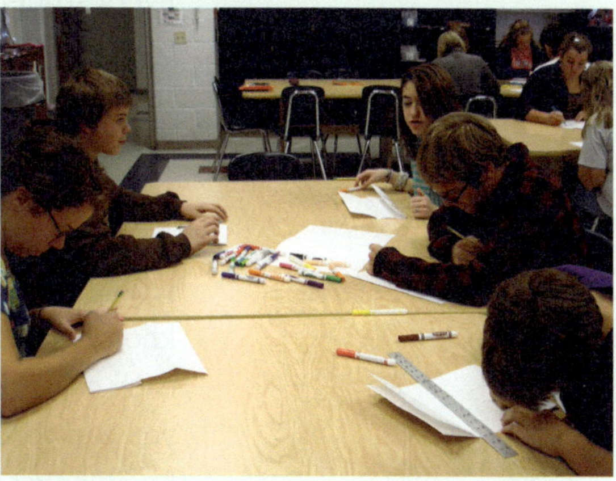

5.17 Collaborative work, such as Exquisite Corpse drawings, expands students' thinking as they see how others solve the same challenge in varied ways. Photo by Heather L. R. Fountain.

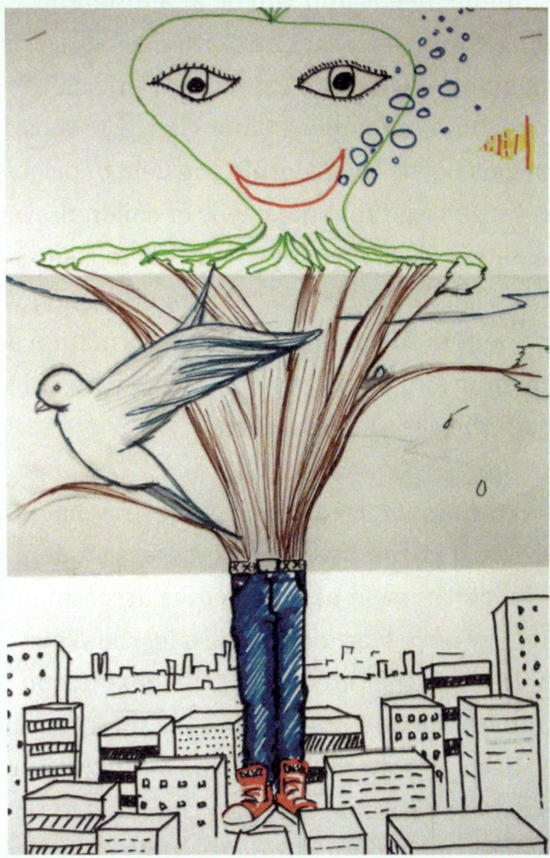

5.18 Three students created this collaborative drawing. Photo by Heather L. R. Fountain.

For students with specific disabilities, their readiness and ability level can often be gauged by reading their Individualized Education Plan, talking with specialists such as support teachers or paraprofessionals who work with the students on a regular basis, and consulting with the special education teacher, or in some cases, by discreetly talking with the students or their care providers.

Every student has unique needs and will be at a different place on the learning spectrum. Students with disabilities can range from those who have what are considered "invisible" disabilities that you would not notice at first glance, to those who have more obvious needs. Even within the field of disability education, it is always stressed that the needs of children, even with the same disability, will vary greatly. The key is to get to know each child and what he or she is capable of doing and what each struggles with, and then gather as much information as you can through reading and talking to specialists who are knowledgeable about the specific disability.

The "Exit Card" is a commonly used assessment tool that is both quick and flexible. You can use it to pre-assess students' knowledge about a topic or use it as a formative assessment to determine what they have learned during a lesson. This information can help guide the direction of the next lesson and will ensure that students clearly understand the information you will present or have presented. To use this strategy, write on the board or ask out loud a question that is related to the information you will be presenting during the next class if you are pre-assessing, or a question that summarizes a point that you made during the class if you are looking for a formative assessment. Have students answer the question on a note card and hand it to you as they leave. As you receive the cards, you

TRY THIS

Exit Card

At the end of this chapter, write a response on an index card to the following prompts:

1 Of the pre-assessment strategies presented in this chapter, choose one that would work best with your students.

2 What two new strategies will you try?

can rapidly scan them and sort them into categories or levels of understanding by placing them in groups between your fingers. This method helps you quickly gain information and ensures that you maximize your time by sorting on the spot.

Using Students' Learning Styles

Proactive design that uses learning styles or multiple intelligences preferences can begin in two different ways: one is to pre-assess students so both you and they know what their strengths are; a second is for you to design a lesson without pre-assessment that intentionally includes elements that relate to all four learning styles (visual, kinesthetic, verbal, and auditory). Although the first option is highly recommended because you can tailor pre-assessments to the specific population you are working with, sometimes it is not convenient or possible to pre-assess students. Also, it is important to note that once you know your students' learning styles, that does not mean you need to design all your lessons using that information. This is just one tool to help you find ways to connect your students with learning.

Pre-assessing learning styles or multiple intelligences preferences can be extremely beneficial in helping you to create lessons and a classroom environment that supports different ways of learning. It also helps you consider your students' natural modes of processing information, which will help them learn more efficiently and effectively. In fact, a study by R. J. Sternberg and his associates found that when students are taught in a way that includes all learning styles, whether students choose how they learn or not, they attain high levels of understanding.[5]

During the first day of class when you are getting to know your students' interests, discussing class rules, and introducing yourself, you could have students use a learning style pre-assessment to discover how they learn best. For some students this is an empowering moment. They begin to realize that they learn best through a particular modality or modalities and that some ways of learning are easy for some people, but difficult for others.

Some students will have a clear learning style while others might overlap in two or more areas. I have often kept track of learning styles by having students mark down their scores in their art folder during the first day of class. They first have to take a pre-assessment and identify their learning style or styles, then write their score (from a pre-assessment found in the Appendix, such as A.5.3a and b) for each learning style on the inside of their folder, with their top scoring learning style on the outside top-right corner. Having this information on the inside of their folder helped them, as sometimes I would have them self-group by their learning preference or with someone who had a different preference. In addition, having their top learning preference on the outside of their folder was a tool for me to use when grouping; I could look in our class box and quickly sort their folders into groups according to differences or preferences.

Many learning-style inventories have been created for use with varied ages, from young children through adults. Some are written and others are given orally and have students draw or color in smiley, ho-hum, or sad faces as their responses. See worksheets in the Appendix for the examples *What's My Learning Style?* (A.5.3a and A.5.3b) and *Oral Learning Style Inventory* (A.5.4). Learning style inventories need to have a significant amount of questions related to each learning style and need to be worded in a way that is not leading or too vague in order to get the most accurate answers.

Using Learning Styles without Pre-Assessment

When you design curriculum using learning styles, you begin to consider including choices that relay information through visual, written, kinesthetic, and auditory means. Your overall plan should include modes of communication and interaction from all four learning styles if you want all types of learners to engage in the lesson.

When planning, consider the following questions:

1. Are there elements such as pictures, maps, graphic organizers, or other visual aids in this lesson to help visual learners connect with key concepts and skills?
2. Are there opportunities in your lessons for students to move, use their hands, or interact, which help kinesthetic learners connect with key concepts and skills?
3. Have you provided written information, opportunities for written reflection, or an opportunity to conduct research to help written learners connect with key concepts and skills?
4. Have you included elements such as music, oral directions, discussions, or conversations in your lessons to help auditory learners connect with key concepts or skills?

If your lessons incorporate varied types of interaction that include visual, kinesthetic, written, and auditory modes, you will increase the likelihood of your students connecting, processing, and applying knowledge.

Using learning styles to create choices or groups within your lessons is another way to design proactively. The following chart and examples will provide some options that would be attractive to each type of learner.

STRATEGY GUIDE

Strategies and Options for Processing Information by Learning Style (Four Square)

Visual

Maps	Video/Podcasts
Posters	Story Mapping
Timelines	Graphic Organizers
Collages	Visualization
Photographs	3-D Modeling
Sketching	Watching Demonstrations

Kinesthetic

Acting	Demonstrating a Task
Sculpting	Experimenting
Role Playing	Showing by Example
Creating	Collecting Items
Miming	Distributing Items
Dancing	Gestures or Actions

Written

Reports	Journals/Blogs
Reading	Letters
Note-Taking	Labeling Items
Poetry	Directions to Post
Stories	Research Papers
Checklists	Newsletters

Auditory

Podcasts	Music (Rap)/Singing
Speeches	Oral Directions
Presentations	Asking Questions
Debates	Mnemonic Devices
Interviews	Commercials
Recordings	News Broadcasts

See Appendix for *Planning for Differentiation by Learning Style Using Four Square* (A.5.5a), *Planning for Differentiation Using Four Square—Example* (A.5.5b), and a blank *Planning for Differentiation by Learning Style (Four Square)* (A.5.5.c) sheet for your own lesson.

TRY THIS

Elementary—ASK ME! List

After students take a multiple intelligences test and obtain their results, have them create a list of the things they are good at and the topics they feel they know a lot about. Have them place this list in their art folder. This will help accomplish three goals:

1. It will serve as a reminder to students that, even though they may not feel confident at something they will be doing in art class, they are good at many things.
2. When students get stuck and cannot think of an idea for their artwork, they can refer to their list to help them gather ideas.
3. If students in the class need help, they can look at their peers' "Ask Me" sheets to find assistance instead of going to the teacher all the time.

Ask Me!

I am good at...

I know a lot about...

Pre-assessing Multiple Intelligences (MI) Preferences

When considering students' learning styles and how their brains think, process, and acquire knowledge, the use of Gardner's multiple intelligences theory provides a more detailed assessment than a traditional learning styles inventory such as the Four Square. Gardner's research helps you to understand students through eight distinct intelligence areas. There are many MI pre-assessments available that students can complete in a short amount of time.[6] One of my favorites, the "Birmingham Grid for Learning Multiple Intelligences," can be found online. This MI test allows individuals to answer a series of questions online and, when completed, will provide a visual graphic of the results and a password, so that the results can be revisited at any time.

Whether you use a paper test like *WOW! You Are Smart* (see Appendix, A.5.6) or an online variation, you will get a quick glance at what type of learning preferences your students have. The results will help students see, often for the first time, what their strengths are and in which areas they need work.

Using Multiple Intelligences Preferences with or without Pre-Assessment

You can assign specific choices to students or group them in various ways according to their MI preferences. If you do not know your students' MI preferences, you can still use the multiple intelligences theory to create student self-selected choices and vary instruction in ways that will meet all learning styles. Some teachers use the eight MI areas to guide their creation of choice boards where students have many options from which to choose. Chapter 7 will provide more detailed information about choice boards.

STRATEGY GUIDE

Ideas for Differentiating Instruction by Multiple Intelligences Preferences

The following guide will assist you in thinking about what choices and artists could be attractive to students with each type of intelligence preference.

Verbal/Linguistic (Say It)
Artist Suggestions: Robert Indiana, Jenny Holzer, Bruce Nauman, Ben Rubin, and Mark Hansen

Poetry, debates, monologue, reader's theater, idioms, onomatopoeia, word puzzles, creative writing, newspaper production, diaries, journals, drama, word games, speeches, and presentations

Logical/Mathematical (Count It)
Artist Suggestions: Frederick Lynch, Alma Thomas, M.C. Escher, Claes Oldenburg, and Bridget Riley

Timelines, problem solving, analogies, pattern identification, predictions, creating flowcharts, counting, sorting and grouping, determining scale, logic/reasoning games, justifying answers

Visual/Spatial (Picture It)
Artist Suggestions: Chris Williams, Louise Nevelson, Donna Howell-Sickles, and Harriet Powers

Dioramas, maps, sketching, hands-on building, manipulation, storyboards, film/video, photography, visual-thinking maps, sculptures, graphic organizers, color mixing and identification

Bodily/Kinesthetic (Move It)
Artist and Event Suggestions: Alexander Calder, Faith Ringgold, Vollis Simpson, and Baltimore's Kinetic Sculpture Race

Dance, gestures, Simon Says, interactive directions, making up songs with hand motions, sculpting, identifying and creating rich textures, acting things out, tapping out patterns seen in artworks, building models

Musical/Rhythmical (Hum It)
Artist Suggestions: Wassily Kandinsky, George Rhoads, George Harriman, Marcus Wuebker, and Dorothea Rockburne

Rhymes and raps, background music, creating songs, using music to suggest the tone, mood, and setting of an artwork, using songs to remember directions, tool care and facts, artists and artworks that include sound

Naturalistic/Environmental (Investigate It)
Artist Suggestions: Charley Harper, Robert Bateman, Jan Jäger, John Dahlsen, and Andy Goldsworthy

Nature walks and talks, studying animals and plants, classification of wildlife, outdoor lessons, collecting natural materials, using natural materials, environmental issues

continued on next page

Interpersonal (Lead It)

Artist Suggestions: Banksy, Yvonne Jacquette, Leonardo da Vinci, Red Grooms, and Jaune Quick-to-See Smith

Group projects, interviews, role-playing, project manager, conflict resolution/negotiating skills, seeing things from others' viewpoints, service learning, mentoring others, peer coaching

Intrapersonal (Reflect on It)

Artist Suggestions: Jacob Lawrence, George Segal, Lola Álvarez Bravo, Norman Rockwell, and Frank Warren

Personality collage, self-portraits, family projects, personal journal reflections, mind maps, any self-focused topic, letters to self, autobiographies, sharing personal opinions, identity assignments

In the Appendix, see the *Planning for Differentiation by Multiple Intelligences Preference* worksheets (A.5.7a and A.5.7b), an MI preferences planning example, and a blank MI planning sheet.

Conclusion

There are many ways to create a positive learning environment for students, but getting to know them as individuals is the first step in the process. This chapter has covered several methods of pre-assessment that will help you discover who your students are and how they learn. We have also explored how to plan using pre-assessment and learning-style information to foster greater connection between you and your students, and between your students and what they are learning. Take some time now to think about your classroom environment. Read the Think Point sidebar for factors that can affect student learning, and consider how each currently adds to or detracts from learning in your class.

THINK POINT

Factors That Affect Learning

- Think about how you currently use the factors below in positive ways to help your students learn.
- Are there any adjustments you can make to your learning environment to help students connect in better ways?
- What factors seem out of your control? Who can help you with these items?

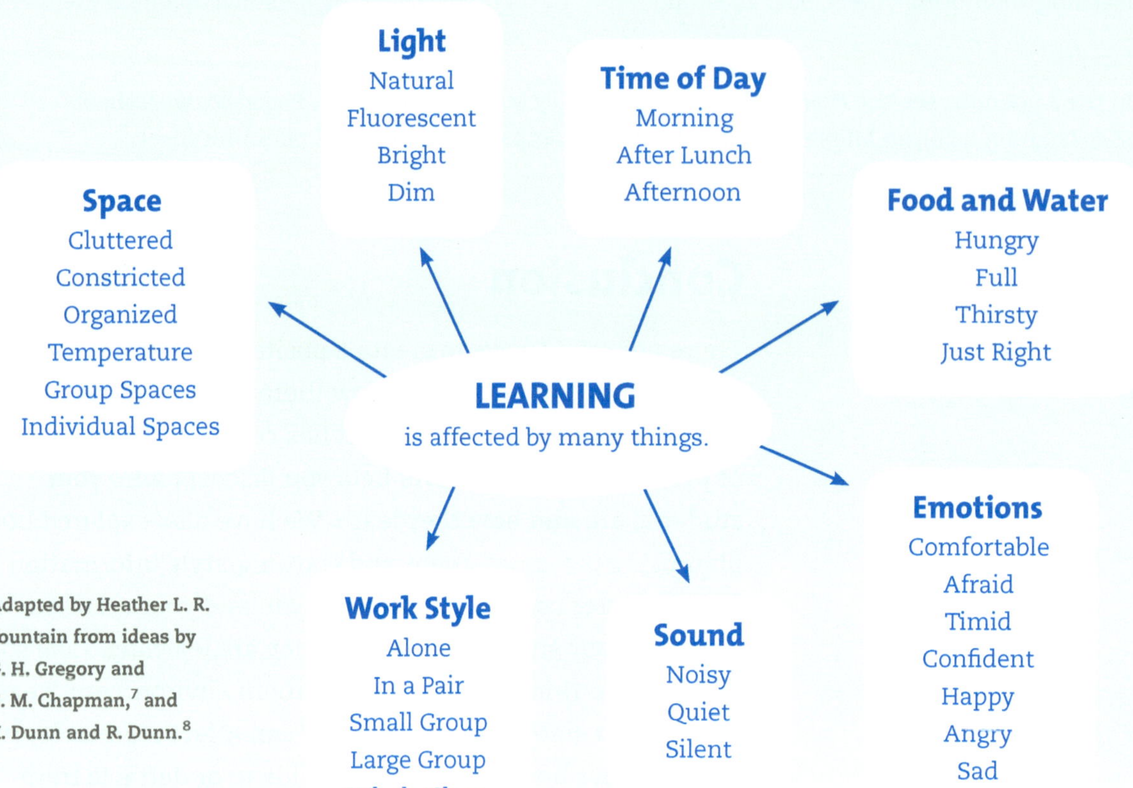

Adapted by Heather L. R. Fountain from ideas by G. H. Gregory and C. M. Chapman,[7] and K. Dunn and R. Dunn.[8]

REFLECTION & PRACTICE

Gathering Data

1 **Proactive Design** Think of a lesson that you will teach soon. Apply the KWL chart, Visual Thinking Map, or the Frayer Diagram, to help you pre-assess what knowledge your students already have about the lesson topic. Adjust your lesson plan to reflect the needs of your students.

If some students already know some of the content you were planning on teaching, add in another direction for those who are ready to move beyond the basic knowledge. If other students don't seem to have enough knowledge, create an activity that will help prepare them to move on.

2 **Learning Styles** Choose a lesson plan (it can be the same one from the last exercise) and a blank copy of *Planning for Differentiation by Learning Style (Four Square)* from the Appendix (A.5.5c). As you read through your lesson plan, write in each box of the planning sheet the ways in which you have created opportunities for students to engage in the lesson through written, visual, auditory, and kinesthetic means.

This will create a visual map of how students will be asked to engage in the lesson and will allow you to see where deficits are and to adjust your lesson so that all types of learners will find connection within the lesson.

3 **Multiple Intelligences (MI)** Take the *WOW! You Are Smart* test found in the Appendix (A.5.6) or an online variation of the MI test to determine your strengths and weaknesses. Consider how your preferences affect your teaching style?

For instance, I am strong in the area of Visual/Spatial intelligence; I discovered that I often forgot to show images or visuals to illustrate ideas that I mentioned because I assumed that others could see the ideas in their heads, which was not the case for all students. Consider how you might adjust your teaching style or help all types of learners better connect with the content you are teaching.

Notes

1 D. Littky, *The BIG Picture: Education Is Everyone's Business* (Alexandria, VA: Association for Supervision and Curriculum Development, 2004).

2 R. Jackson, "Start Where Your Students Are," *Educational Leadership,* 67, no. 5(2010): pp. 6–10.

3 D. M. Ogle, "K-W-L: A Teaching Model That Develops Active Reading of Expository Text." *The Reading Teacher,* 39, no. 6(1986): pp. 564–570.

4 You can find examples of Frayer's Diagrams and KWL Charts at http://www.ttsd.k12.or.us/tigard-high-school/student-resources/literacy/ls-strategies-2006-2007-2.doc Retrieved on May 18, 2012.

5 R. J. Sternberg, B. Torff, and E. Grigorenko, "Teaching Triarchically Improves Student Achievement," *Journal of Educational Psychology,* 90, no. 3: pp. 374–384.

6 D. Heacox, *Differentiating Instruction in the Regular Classroom: How to Reach and Teach All Learners* (Minneapolis, MN: Free Spirit Publishing, 2002); C. A. Tomlinson. *The Differentiated Classroom: Responding to the Needs of All Learners* (Alexandria, VA: Association for Supervision and Curriculum Development, 1999); C. Chapman and R. King, *Differentiated Assessment Strategies: One Tool Doesn't Fit All* (Thousand Oaks, CA: Corwin Press, 2005); G. H. Gregory, and C. M. Chapman, *Differentiated Instruction Strategies: One Size Doesn't Fit All.* (Thousand Oaks, CA: Corwin Press, 2002).

7 Gregory and Chapman, *Differentiated Instruction Strategies: One Size Doesn't Fit All.*

8 K. Dunn and R. Dunn, "Dispelling Outmoded Beliefs about Student Learning," *Educational Leadership,* 44, no. 6(1987): pp. 55–61.

Chapter 6

Curriculum

"Teachers can change lives with just the right mix of chalk and challenge."

Dr. Joyce A Myers as quoted in *Thank Heavens for Teachers* by H. Exley (Hallmark Company, 1997).

PERSONAL CONNECTIONS

Designing Instruction

As you read, consider the following questions:

1 What have you done in the past to help struggling learners connect when they are having difficulty?

2 How do you currently group students and for what reasons?

3 How much control or choices do students have in directing their own learning in your classroom?

Developing Differentiated Curriculum

An excited buzz filled the air as students moved around the art classroom gathering supplies, checking the choice board, and conferring with peers. "What blue choice did you make? I chose number two because I like poems," Rinnah said to Caleb. "Not me," said Caleb as he looked at his learning menu, "I am making an artist cube."

Upon entering the artroom and hearing this exchange, among others, it took a moment for the visitor to realize that what she first assumed were students not working, were actually students excited and invested in their learning. As she watched the class, she saw how the use of Differentiated Instruction helped to create a community of learners that were able to make decisions and find connections with art learning.

This chapter will examine how you can use various strategies proactively to design strong curriculum that reaches all students through the differentiation of the *content*, *process*, or *product* of the instruction. The examples and information provided will show you how it is possible to assist students in accessing, processing, and demonstrating the knowledge they have gained in various ways, while being engaged and excited about learning in art. The strategies in this chapter are not concepts unique to DI, but when you use them purposefully, they can create powerful differentiated learning experiences.

THEORIES & TERMS

Elements of DI

Content The subject matter you are teaching to students. Content is what the students should know and be able to apply as a result of a unit or lesson study.

Process The lessons, experiences, tasks, and activities that you have designed to aid students in learning about or making sense of the content.

Product Anything that helps students demonstrate what they have come to understand, know, or be able to do as a result of learning.

Tiering Tiering assists you in reaching students who may have different levels of understanding by varying the methods for delivering the same key skills and concepts to all students.

Orbital Studies This strategy focuses on a student's independent investigation of a topic related to the planned curriculum.

Flexible Grouping Purposeful grouping achieves various learning goals without continually grouping students in the same way.

Learning Contracts By negotiating with students to develop specific criteria, tasks, and goals for a lesson, contracts assure that students enjoy an experience specific to their learning needs. Students in a class may have similar contracts, variations on a theme, or completely different contracts.

Learning Centers Stand-alone areas of the room, such as an artist-of-the-week center or a writing center, which allow students to explore a specific topic or theme.

Learning Stations Different areas of the room set up with tasks or learning challenges for students to explore simultaneously. Not all students need to visit each station, but you might assign each to a specific station.

Chunking Breaking down difficult or involved content into smaller bits of information grouped or organized around categories or ideas. This strategy encourages a greater sense of meaning and connection.

Learning Menus A form of a learning contract that allows shared choice-making between the teacher and the students.

MAJOR POINTS

One Step at a Time

It is easy to become overwhelmed when you first start to differentiate instruction, but remember that you do not have to differentiate everything all the time. Start slowly by differentiating one aspect of one lesson.

When trying to decide *what* to differentiate, first consider which area—content, process, or product—makes the most sense to differentiate in your lesson or unit of study. Differentiation should help your students be invested in learning while meeting their learning goals. Once you have made this decision, the chart in the sidebar will assist you in choosing which strategy or tool you will use to differentiate your lesson. You can differentiate all three areas, but it is often helpful to start with just one area.

STRATEGY GUIDE

Methods of Differentiating Instruction

Content

If you want to differentiate the content, consider using:

- Multiple texts or supplementary print resources
- Multiple pieces of artwork
- Varied computer programs
- Varied levels of complexity for a topic
- Contracts
- Group investigation
- Learning centers
- Interest-based choices around a topic (orbital study)

Process

If you want to differentiate the process, consider using:

- Choice boards
- Modeling
- Small group instruction
- Learning centers or stations
- Tiered activities
- Varied methods of instruction
- Varied modes of communication (dance, music, drama, visual art)
- Varied time allotments
- Varied complexity
- Think-Tac-Toe
- Entry points
- Cubing
- ThinkDots
- Graphic organizers
- Learning menus
- RAFTs

Product

If you want to differentiate the product, consider using:

- Tiered product assignments
- Choice boards
- Choice cards
- Negotiating criteria using contracts
- Interest-based choices
- Varied response options
- Group responses
- Think-Tac-Toe
- Entry points
- Cubing
- Think Dots
- Learning Menus
- RAFTs

You can also apply differentiation to extension activities that students, upon completion of their current lesson, can choose as a means to help them extend their learning on the topic you are teaching. You can place an extension center, a choice board, or a set of choice cards in a designated area of the room for students to access.

There are many strategies that can help students to explore learning in different ways or help them to build choice and ownership into a lesson, but each strategy is unique and has different goals. In the next section, we will examine several commonly used strategies in order to help you decide which would be the best match for any given lesson.

Scaffolding

Scaffolding in curriculum, similar to that on a building under construction, provides a supporting framework for people who are trying to accomplish a task. It gives necessary support for a worker or student to build upon previous layers of a structure or body of knowledge. For teachers, scaffolding is a process of focusing on the sequence in which they develop and introduce curriculum to students, so that each part of a lesson builds a foundation for subsequent learning.

For students who find a particular topic or task difficult, or who do not have the prior knowledge or skills they need to move forward, scaffolding helps them reach their goals and grow without being discouraged or feeling left behind. This is a great way to provide extra support to students and ensure that they accomplish critical skills each step of the way.

STRATEGY

How Can You Use Scaffolding to Differentiate?

Scaffolding differentiates the content of a lesson by breaking it down and providing critical information to students who have different levels of skills in and understanding of a topic. It ensures that goals exist for all students to help them grow one step at a time, whether they are challenged, at ease, or gifted in a particular area of learning.

Scaffolding can take many forms, from slightly different assignments to slightly different steps leading up to an assignment. Here is one example: After pre-assessing students on the use of watercolors, I discovered that most of my students had the knowledge I expected they would have, but three students had no experience using this medium. I decided to use a teacher demonstration table as part of the lesson after considering this pre-assessment knowledge.

As teams of students started the first step of their assignment, I called one team at a time up to the demonstration table. With the groups that had previous watercolor experience, I began by asking a few questions to ensure they were aware of my expectations for media care and use. "Can you tell me three things I need to know in order to care for my watercolors?" Following this, I shared a new option for the medium with them and had them try it out on a small sample piece of paper. As they were experimenting, they discussed ways they could use the new option in their artworks.

With the three students who had not used watercolors before, I started by adding water to the paints. As I did this, I asked them what challenges or problems they might have while using watercolors to see if they could make some predictions. They shared some concerns and I showed them a few other challenges they might face, as well as solutions to those challenges. Together, we each made a sampler of watercolor techniques including the new option I had shared with the other groups. This method allowed me to provide these students with the information they needed to succeed, while preserving their dignity.

STRATEGY

How Can You Use Orbital Studies to Differentiate?

Orbital studies differentiate content by providing students with the opportunity to choose their topic based on the curricular theme the class is exploring. This strategy also allows for differentiation of both process and product, as students independently explore their topic and express what they have learned through unique products.

Orbital Studies

Orbital studies do exactly what the name suggests—they revolve around a curriculum theme or topic; but unlike traditional instruction, orbital studies rely on students to choose what they will study.[1] Either groups or individuals can complete orbital studies.

Once you have chosen a curricular topic such as illustration, students can brainstorm a list of related ideas that they would like to explore. You, as the teacher, can augment this list of choices. From this compiled list, students can make a choice of topic (e.g., children's book illustrators, book cover illustrators, the tools used for illustration, greeting card illustration, or how one becomes an illustrator). Next, they can create an investigation plan, form a research question, list criteria for assessment, and decide on a method for presenting their final information and product to at least five peers.

Orbital investigations are primarily independent, and rely on you to become a mentor or guide in helping students along the path of discovery. Students may need your assistance in finding resources, staying on task, using time wisely, measuring progress, and remembering to log their progress and findings.

This method of learning excels in helping students to develop their skills as researchers or investigators while encouraging them to delve into a self-selected aspect of a topic. It also ensures that investment in learning increases, as students are working on *their* lesson and *their* topic, not a topic or lesson that someone else designed. The challenges for the teacher with this type of strategy are the time it takes for students to accomplish (often three or more weeks) and the fact that students work on different tasks at the same time.

STRATEGY

How Can You Use Tiering to Differentiate?

You can use tiering to differentiate process. The content is the same for all students, but they will engage differently with that content at levels matching their readiness. Tiering an assignment or activity might be beneficial when:

- Students have different levels of knowledge as they embark on a project.
- Students have different readiness levels, such as varied writing, reading, or motor skills.
- Students would benefit from engaging in varied learning strategies to help them understand a skill or topic.
- Students need more or less modeling or direct instruction.
- Students need more challenge, complexity, or independence.

Many high school art teachers use this strategy to create a studio atmosphere that encourages students to follow their passions and interests, while delving deeper into their chosen topic.

At an art education conference a few years ago, a teacher approached me who had attended a session I offered on Differentiated Instruction in art the year before. She told me that she now used orbital studies and contracts to negotiate all the work students engaged in during her senior art class. She excitedly shared that DI had changed everything for her and her students. It had helped her to create a "true studio space" in which artists, although working on different ideas and using different media, were providing each other feedback that helped them create the most advanced work she had ever seen in her classes.

For her, the use of DI had fostered a whole new way of teaching that empowered students by giving them the responsibility to design their own classroom experience. She provided mentoring, guidance, direction, and basic standards and expectations for her students, instead of set projects that everyone would work on at the same time in the same way. She explained that on any given day, students might be using five different media in the artroom. At first she was not sure she could handle this level of activity, but she soon realized that the students were engaged and invested. Along with this new energy, students' attitudes changed, leading to increased respect for the art space and the media. They began to care for the media and clean the room as if it belonged to them, which enabled her to use less of her time preparing or cleaning up art supplies.

THINK POINT

Meeting Students' Learning Needs

Tiering is one way to ensure that students with higher levels of knowledge are not bored by repeating tasks in which they are already proficient, while ensuring that struggling learners are given work that is challenging enough for them to grow, but not so challenging that they become overwhelmed and discouraged.

In what ways do you currently meet the needs of students who are excelling in art? In what ways do you meet the needs of students who struggle in art?

Tiering

Early childhood education professor and researcher Lilian Katz once said that when a teacher tries to teach something to the entire class the same way, "chances are, one-third of the kids already know it; one-third will get it; and the remaining third won't. So two-thirds of the children are wasting their time."[2] Tiering, similar to scaffolding, takes into consideration that students have different levels of readiness on any topic.[3] Students meet the same lesson objectives but in ways that ask for appropriate levels of challenge.

Your first step is to decide what your students should know, understand, and be able to accomplish in terms of the instructional topic they have selected. Next, you create an engaging activity or assignment to help students meet the learning goals with a high degree of accomplishment. From that activity, you can develop multiple versions that take into consideration students' readiness and provide options with various degrees of difficulty. These versions of the activity could vary in complexity, abstraction, or open-endedness of the assignment.

In order to tier a lesson or activity by complexity, develop an option that helps students work with the same concepts but incorporates more complexity; then develop an option in which students can work on the same concepts with less complexity. This method leads to three tiers or levels of learning. Usually, the teacher assigns each student a tier to work on, but you could also have students choose a particular option if you see that this would fit their needs. This strategy helps ensure that all students reach their learning goals and are appropriately challenged, not under- or over-challenged. In the Appendix, you will find examples of tiered lessons that consider an artwork's setting (see worksheets A.6.1a, b, and c).

STRATEGY

How Can You Use Flexible Grouping to Differentiate?

You can use flexible grouping to differentiate the process of how students will be exploring, working, and interacting with the content of a lesson or topic.

DID YOU KNOW?

Grouping

How you group students can have a significant effect on their learning:

- Struggling or low-performing learners have more difficulties when grouped with other low-performing learners.
- High-ability learners have limited growth when grouped together.[4]

Flexible Grouping

One of the hallmarks of a teacher using Differentiated Instruction is flexibility, and this is critical when it comes to grouping students. Flexible grouping is instructional grouping that changes as needed to optimize learning experiences. Students could be put into one or a combination of the following instructional groups: individual, partners, small group, whole class, by similarities, by differences, by personalities, by student choice, or random. Ongoing evaluations help you identify and monitor the need for grouping and regrouping throughout the lesson or unit.

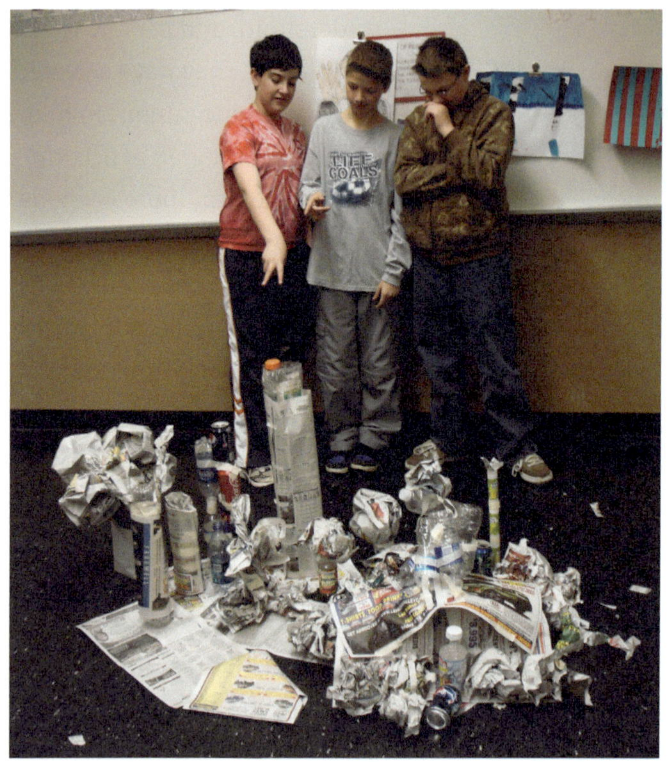

6.1 When working in groups, students learn from others' perspectives. In this case, the project engineer points out two final adjustments that the group could make to their product before it is assessed. Photo by Heather L. R. Fountain.

TIP

Group Interaction

When students work in a group, it is easy for one student to end up working harder than others. To avoid this, be sure to set clear expectations for group interaction. This could include an assigned task for each group member such as timekeeper, recorder, note taker, sketch artist, or Internet fact checker. When the group works together for a long time or on a specific project, have students peer assess and self-assess the contributions that each has made to the group. They could even turn in a progress report part way through a long-term assignment.

Sometimes you can use grouping to place students with similar learning styles or interests together. At other times, you may want to group students by differences. This is a technique that often works best when students have different learning styles. As a group completes a task together, each student in it will have a unique strength to offer. This often leads students to deeper understanding or discovery because their peers bring up things some members would not have thought of on their own. One important tip is to change grouping often, so that students are not continually working in the same way or with the same people.

Sometimes whole-group instruction is necessary, but the use of flexible grouping has been found to:[5]

- Reduce the effect of cliques by varying students' work partners.
- Create opportunities for students to learn about others that they may not work with by choice.
- Promote student independence.
- Help students to learn concepts while acquiring interpersonal skills.
- Teach students how to negotiate differences with others.
- Assist teachers in providing instruction that addresses specific learning needs.
- Vary instruction to add an element of excitement for students.
- Foster an atmosphere where students become more confident.

TIP

Whole-Group Instruction

Whole-group instruction is most effective when you are:

1 Building a sense of community in the class.

2 Introducing new skills, topics, or concepts.

3 Conducting discussions about important content.

4 Answering questions that might be relevant to the whole group.

STRATEGY

How Can You Use Contracts to Differentiate?

Contracts can differentiate the content, the process, and/or the product of a lesson. For another example, see discussion of the Freedom Choice Board contract in chapter 7 on p. 159.

- Prevent students from always being in the same level or type of group.
- Create an opportunity for students to learn from each others' perspectives and experiences.
- Challenge students to use their less-preferred multiple intelligences areas.

Learning Contracts

Learning contracts are agreements made between teachers and students that provide students with some control over their learning goals. Contracts can take many forms, but are often used in one of two ways. In the first option, students fill out a teacher-designed contract that helps them, in conjunction with their teacher, design a lesson around their own interests. The second option offers students the freedom to choose how they wish to demonstrate their knowledge that is a result of teacher- or student-designed choices.

One value of contracts is that they provide choices and help students to have greater investment in their learning. In addition, contracts provide students with opportunities to seek knowledge and to hold themselves accountable for their time and the quality of their work, and to problem solve the steps they must follow to complete their contractual assignments.

This is a great strategy to use in an advanced art class or AP class where students might have diverse artistic needs that necessitate a more individualized class structure. In addition, contracts pair well with choice boards. After creating a choice board, students identify on their contracts which choices they will complete.

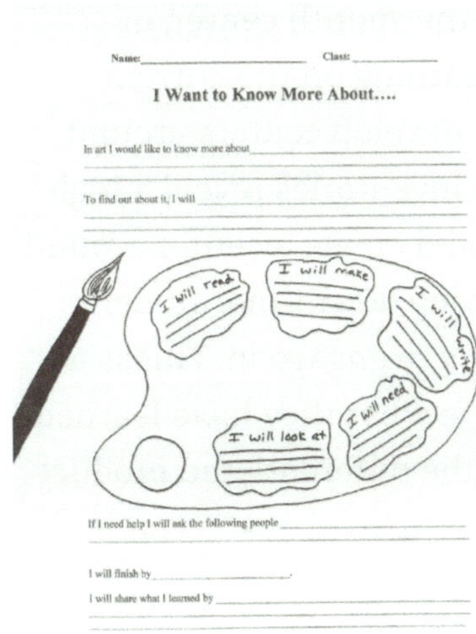

Name: ____________ Class: ________

I Want to Know More About….

In art I would like to know more about ____________

To find out about it, I will ____________

I will read

I will make

I will write

I will need

I will look at

If I need help I will ask the following people ____________

I will finish by ____________.

I will share what I learned by ____________

6.2 Art contracts can help teachers and students negotiate projects and transfer ownership of learning to the student. Created by Heather L. R. Fountain.

STRATEGY

How Can You Use Stations and Centers to Differentiate?

By engaging students in different ways at each station or center, you can differentiate the process of instruction. Its use may also result in a differentiation of the product, if each station requires a different method to demonstrate understanding.

Often learning contracts include:

- Tasks to complete.
- A timetable for completion.
- Criteria for successful completion of work.
- Working parameters such as consequences for inability to meet contract agreements.
- Both student and teacher signatures of agreement.

Centers and Stations

At first glance, centers and stations seem the same—students working on a specific task at different locations in the classroom—but they differ in one major way: as students visit them, stations work together to help students explore or learn about one topic; whereas centers focus on individual unrelated topics and do not require students to visit all of them.

Stations are an efficient way to have students work in small groups and explore many facets of a topic. For example, when beginning a unit on social issues, you could create five or six stations, basing each one on a topic that engages students in a current issue and introduces them to different artists who create artwork relevant to that social issue. In this scenario, students explore all stations and encounter many artists in a short amount of time, giving them enough information to begin delving into the unit topic in depth. All students in the class can visit every station, but you can also group students and have them explore just one or two stations.

Unlike stations, centers stand alone. That does not mean that they are unrelated to the current topic you are teaching, but they could be. For example, you could create one center for students to use, such as an artist-of-the-month center, or a center that helps extend student learning on the current topic they are studying. You can also develop centers around student interests. If student-interest inventories reveal a high level of interest in animation, you could create a center around that topic for students to explore during downtime. Students can even create centers for their peers to engage in. This is a great way for students to demonstrate what they have learned about a topic, and it could be one of the differentiated product choices you offer to students.

TRY THIS

Middle School Printmaking Stations

Creating stations can be a great way to help students explore a wide variety of ideas in a short amount of time. Try using stations to begin a lesson that helps students gain an overview of a medium or type of art such as printmaking. You can provide written directions and media at each station so that students can learn about and try out one type of printmaking technique such as gelatin, collograph, stamping, engraving, or monoprinting. (See Appendix sheets A.6.1a–c for sample printmaking station ideas.) After a certain amount of time, have students rotate to other stations until they have visited all of them.

After this exploration, students can create proposals or learning contracts for their own printmaking series. They will need to decide on a topic for their series, which printmaking techniques they will use, and justifications for the choices they have made.

Printmaking Proposal—My Series

Name:

The topic or theme of my series will be:

I think this is an important theme because:

I will use the three following printmaking techniques to complete my series:

1. **2.** **3.**

I will know that my series is completed to the best of my ability when the following things have happened:

1. **2.** **3.** **4.**

I will need to complete the following research to help me accomplish my series:

I am responsible for meeting the terms of this contract and completing all my work to the best of my ability by the deadline. If I do not meet the terms of this contract by the deadline, I understand that I will have to complete this assignment on my own time.

Signature: **Date:**

continued on next page

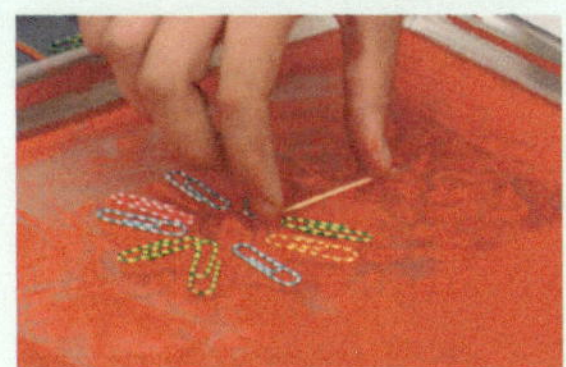

6.3 A student works with found objects to create a print at the monoprinting station. Photo by Heather L. R. Fountain.

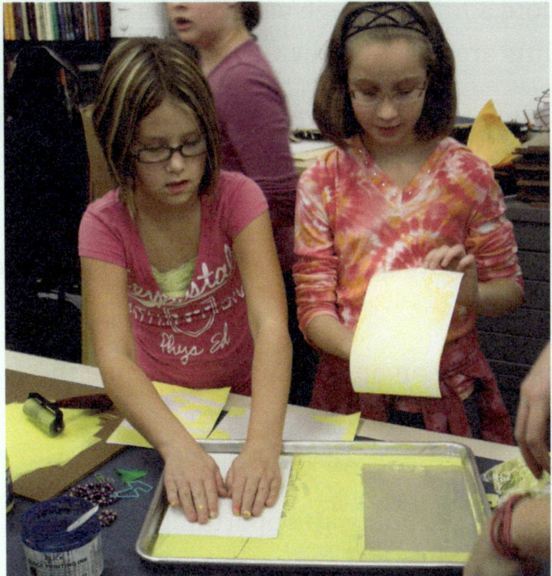

6.4 Two students work on their prints at the gelatin station. Photo by Heather L. R. Fountain.

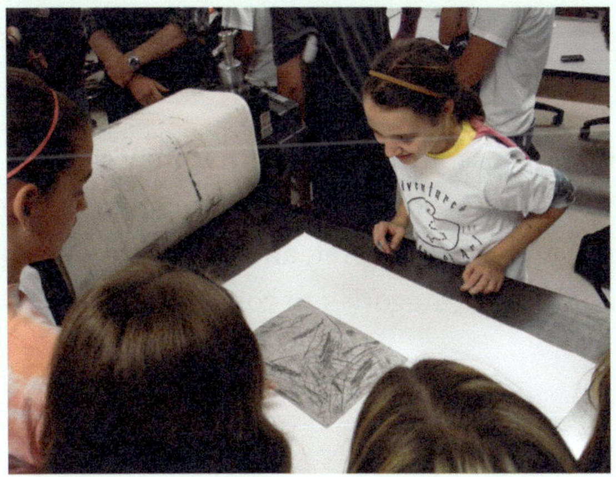

6.5 Students watch as their team-created etching is revealed at the etching station. Photo by Heather L. R. Fountain.

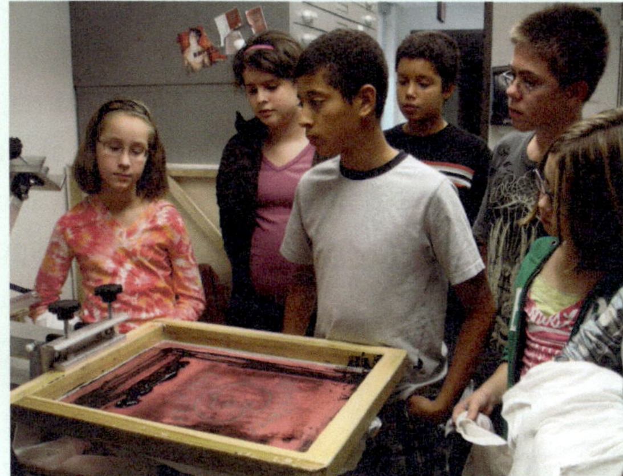

6.6 After a demonstration, students screen print their own shirts. Photo by Heather L. R. Fountain.

What is differentiated in this lesson?

The content is partially differentiated. Although all students will explore the printmaking stations and learn about printmaking, they will make individual choices about the types of printmaking they will use to complete their series. Experimenting at each of the stations will help students make decisions about what type of technique might best fit their style, match their topic or theme, or allow them to use a method that interests them the most.

The product is differentiated, allowing students to make specific thoughtful decisions about a topic or theme around which they want to organize their work. Students can take complete ownership of the theme and can choose appropriate items that are related to their interests, backgrounds, or other ideas they have.

Entry Points

Entry points, a strategy created by Howard Gardner, honors individual learning styles by offering five different ways to engage students in a topic.[6] By creating a choice or question that corresponds with each of the five entry-point areas, students can explore a topic through a specific lens. The five entry points are described by Gardner as:

1. Aesthetic, providing an opportunity to respond to the formal or sensory qualities of a subject or work of art.

2. Experiential, providing an opportunity to respond to a subject or work of art through physical action and hands-on experience.

3. Foundational, providing an opportunity to examine the philosophy and vocabulary associated with a subject or artwork.

4. Logical-Quantitative, providing an opportunity to use the scientific method or a numeric approach to the exploration of a subject or artwork.

5. Narrational, providing an opportunity to consider and then create a story or narrative about the subject or artwork.

Cubing

The strategy of cubing has some elements that may seem familiar to Bloom's Taxonomy or Feldman's components of art criticism—describe, analyze, interpret, and evaluate—except that it has a few additional categories to consider.

STRATEGY

How Can You Use Entry Points to Differentiate?

You can use entry points to differentiate the process of how students engage with a topic. Each entry-point choice provides a different perspective for students to consider and, possibly, a different product to create as a demonstration of their thoughts and ideas.

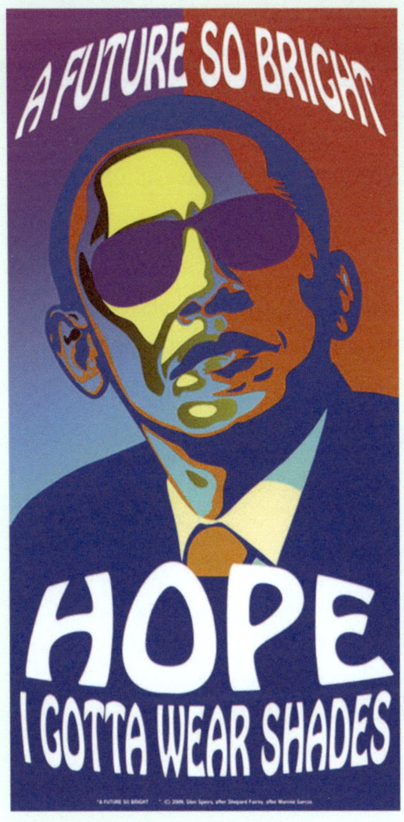

Entry Points

Narrational Read artist Shepard Fairey's statements about his Obama posters. Write a short narrative on the transformation in the posters' messages over the course of the first Obama presidency.

Logical-Quantitative Investigate how many artistic images of President Obama exist. What percentage features the theme of hope?

Foundational What was the artist's intent when emphasizing a single word such as hope on a poster?

Aesthetic Use the four components of art criticism (describe, interpret, analyze, evaluate) to discuss the visual qualities of this image.

Experiential Create your own graphic image of someone who inspires you. Include text that emphasizes how that person makes you feel.

6.7 *Entry Point Example.* **Created by Heather L. R. Fountain. Image used by permission of artist Glenn Speirs.**

THEORIES & TERMS

Bloom's Taxonomy

Did you know that Bloom's Taxonomy, created in 1956 by a group of educational psychologists lead by Benjamin Bloom, is a way to classify levels of intellectual behavior? However, that is not where the story ends; during the 1990s, a former student of Bloom's, Lorin Anderson, worked with a new group of psychologists to update the taxonomy and make it more relevant to the twenty-first century.[7] Many educators use Bloom's Taxonomy when creating lesson objectives. Each level of the taxonomy from *Knowledge,* at the bottom of the pyramid through *Synthesis* at the top, signifies greater levels of learning achievement.

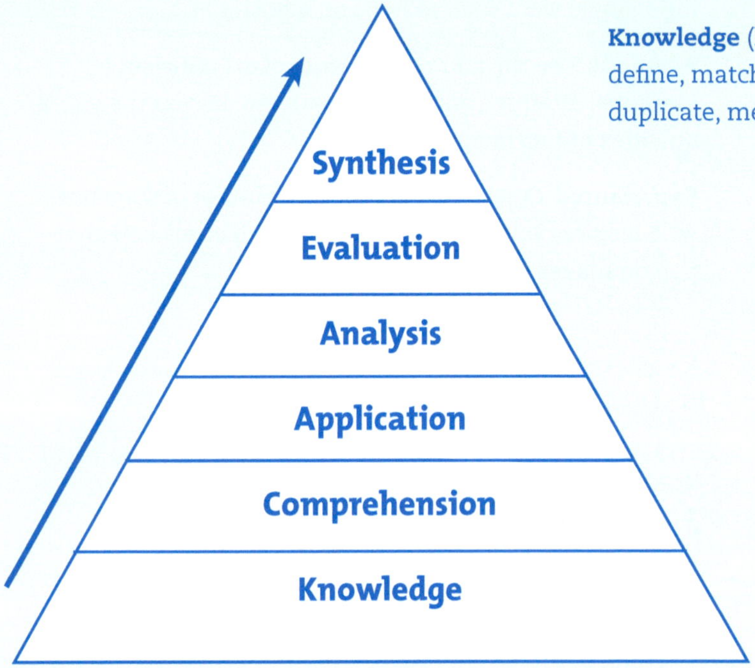

6.8 ***Bloom's Taxonomy.*** **Drawn by Heather L. R. Fountain.**

Synthesis (create): assemble, design, invent, compose, rewrite, develop, formulate

Evaluation (judge): critique, justify, judge, recommend, predict, assess, decide, evaluate, rate

Analysis (break apart): examine, compare, contrast, group, sequence, order, categorize, question, test

Application (apply): use, illustrate, choose, solve, research, show, perform, demonstrate, construct

Comprehension (understand): describe, explain, summarize, translate, paraphrase, retell, interpret, discuss

Knowledge (know or remember): tell, list, define, match, name, identify, recognize, repeat, duplicate, memorize

In cubing, students consider a subject from six different perspectives: description, comparison, association, analysis, application, and argumentation. Cubing was originally intended to help students consider a story, a topic, or film from many vantage points and then generate ideas prior to writing. You can apply this same concept to any piece of artwork to help students dig in deep and look beyond the surface. Educator Elizabeth Neeld, who created cubing, describes each of the following categories of the strategy, which she states should be followed in order, unlike Feldman's model, which can be used in varied order:

- **Description** Factually describe anything that relates to the five senses (touch, taste, smell, hear, or see).
- **Comparison** Compare and contrast an item to something else, and list the similarities and differences.
- **Association** Identify anything you associate with the topic or object such as things that you remember or are reminded of when you see or hear about the topic or object.
- **Analysis** Consider the formal parts of the story, topic, or object of focus that make it whole. For a piece of artwork, you could look at how the artist used the elements and principles of art to convey an emotion, idea, message, or tell a story.
- **Application** State how you could apply the topic, subject, or information found in the artwork. For instance, after analyzing political or propaganda posters, students could apply elements from these works by appropriating them for their own work to help successfully convey an important message.
- **Argumentation** Discuss the topic, subject, or artwork from all angles by discussing both its strengths and weaknesses.

STRATEGY

How Does Cubing Differentiate?

By providing six different perspectives to consider, cubing differentiates the process by which students engage with a topic.

To create your cube, insert one cubing choice in each box and cut out the entire shape. Fold on the solid lines and glue or tape the small tabs in place.

Compare and contrast the *Mona Lisa* with *The Pow Wow Princess in the Process of Acculturation*

Describe what you see.

How has the artist used line, color, shape, and form within this work?

Why do you think the artist felt it was important to create this work?

How could it be used to educate others?

What parts of this work seem most successful and why?

Are there any parts you would change? What are they? If not, why not?

Describe in detail something that you are reminded of when you look at this piece.

6.9 *Cubing Example*

Created by Heather L. R. Fountain.

An enjoyable way to use this strategy is to place one category or a question related to each category on each side of an actual cube. Students can toss or roll the cube to reveal the response option they will complete. Students can do this in a large circle, at a table, or individually. In the Appendix, you will find a template (see sheet A.6.2) that will help you to begin creating your own cube.

ThinkDots

ThinkDots help students review or extend their thinking on a topic that they have already studied.[8] You can also use this approach as a review strategy to test students' retention of a previously explored topic. To create ThinkDots, you will need to develop six choices of varying complexity related to your chosen topic objectives. You can use each level of Bloom's Taxonomy as a guide to ensure that the choices range from basic knowledge questions to those that require higher-level thinking skills. Each choice will become a ThinkDot card with dots on it ranging from one to six.

To use the cards, students roll one of a pair of dice to reveal a number between one and six. The number revealed on the die will correspond with the ThinkDot choice on which they will work. You can group this set of cards together with a string, pipe cleaner, or notebook ring. You could even create multiple sets of cards and hang them in a specific place in the room or give a set to each table. You can laminate the cards so that they will last longer.

You could create a center where you display choices on a bulletin board. Each choice could have a pocket behind it with copies of that specific choice card in it for students to take back to their seats. Having a personal choice card helps students with memory issues stay on task, and it also helps avoid traffic jams and subsequent behavior issues around the center. With this option, students could visit the center, roll the die, take the corresponding choice card, and return to their tables to begin their task. When a student finishes one task, he or she can roll the die and work on another ThinkDot choice card.

A variation of this strategy is to create sets of ThinkDot cards based on learning styles, interests, or readiness, and then assign groups of students to work with one specific set of cards.

STRATEGY

How Can You Use ThinkDots to Differentiate?

You can use ThinkDots to differentiate the process by which students engage in a topic either through your selection or their own.

Look around the classroom. Find and draw three patterns that you see.

Create five patterns using items from the grab bag. Draw and color your patterns on a piece of black paper using gel pens or construction paper crayons.

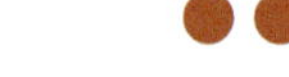

Draw and color five things from nature that show pattern.

Create a poem that has a pattern in it and create a patterned border around your poem that fits with the topic you have written about.

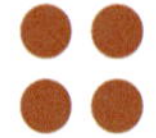

Create a new package design for a crayon company. Use at least three patterns in your design and carefully consider how color will be used in your final image.

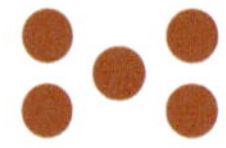

You are the teacher today! Place an "X" over the incorrect patterns on the ABABA sheet. Redraw the patterns to fix them so your students will know the correct answers.

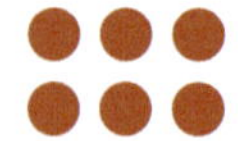

6.10 *ThinkDot Example: Pattern.* ThinkDots add choice to learning, while also allowing teachers the flexibility to vary the levels of complexity and transition within the choices. Modified and used with permission from Marcie Khuns.

STRATEGY

What Does Chunking Differentiate?

Chunking can be an effective way to differentiate the content that students are learning and help them gain a depth of knowledge about one aspect of a topic. Chunking can also lead to the differentiation of the process and the product if you encourage each team or student to search for knowledge about their specific chunk in different ways and then teach their peers in varied ways as well.

Chunked Learning

Chunked learning, often called chunking or jigsaw, is a strategy that helps students consider large amounts of information in a short amount of time.[9] This is accomplished by taking a large topic or body of information and assigning small chunks of the topic to individual students or student groups to learn about and explore. Each student or group becomes the expert in their area of the topic and shares what they have discovered with the whole class. The benefits of this strategy are:

1. Less time is needed to consider large amounts of information.
2. Students lead the instruction instead of the teacher.
3. Students become experts in one area of a topic.
4. Stress is more manageable for students due to the reduced amount of information they need to consider.
5. More class time is gained for other activities and topics.

Chunking Example

In the school where I taught, the third grade students learned about ancient Egypt. In our curriculum guide, it stated that they had to consider the following topics:

- Leadership in government and religion.
- Culture as reflected in food, music, dress, and burial customs.
- Life in terms of social status, education, jobs, and roles.
- Art and architecture of homes, monuments, and palaces.

This seemed like a huge order at first, but chunking made it more manageable. In self-selected groups, students explored their chosen topic and became experts. Then, each group taught their classmates in a fun and interactive way. This ensured that the whole class learned about all areas of the ancient Egypt curriculum by the end of the lesson.

STRATEGY

What do Learning Menus Differentiate?

Menus are a great way to differentiate the products students will create to demonstrate what they have learned about their chosen content area. The menu provides you with the control that ensures students engage in choices that challenge them, while it provides the freedom for them to make their own choices based on their interests.

Learning Menus

Learning menus help you provide choices for students while ensuring that they complete the topics or skills you feel are essential to their learning experience. Often a menu will consist of three categories: appetizer, main course, and dessert. One category will have a specific chosen assignment that all students must complete, while the other two categories consist of options from which students can choose.

Similar to dining from a prix fixe menu at a restaurant, at least one item is chosen by the teacher or the student in each category to make a complete "meal" or assignment. The beauty of this strategy is that it allows for student choice and, therefore, investment in assignments, but it also ensures that you can help your students focus on specific skills or tasks that will help to challenge them and help them to meet their learning goals.

STRATEGY

What Does Think-Tac-Toe Differentiate?

Think-Tac-Toe differentiates the process of engaging in a topic. Depending on the design of your Think-Tac-Toe, you could address different levels of readiness, student interests, or learning styles.

Think-Tac-Toe

The Think-Tac-Toe strategy is another idea that builds choice into learning while ensuring students explore key concepts and skills. Create a grid similar to Tic-Tac-Toe with nine blocks. You can design each row across to represent one concept related to the lesson, such as color, emotion, or composition. Then, place three choices related to the topic in each row. You can tier these topics to meet students' levels of readiness, or design them around interests or learning styles such as

The Style It Café

This is a restaurant with its own style.

In each category you will discover menu items; sometimes you will need to make a choice of your own and sometimes the chef has specifically chosen an item just for you. Place your name on your menu card and be sure to circle your choice in each category. Please choose at least one appetizer, one main course and one dessert.

APPETIZERS

Compare and Contrast Nachos

Check out two folders from the art library: (a.) Mark Bradford and Beatriz Milhazes or (b.) Julie Morgan and Frank Gehry or (c.) Usher and the BEPs. Using a Venn diagram, compare and contrast the style of their art. Be sure to focus on colors, lines, shapes, mood, etc.

Portfolio Hot Wings

Open your portfolio and look at your own artwork. Write a rich description of your style in at least two complete paragraphs. In a third paragraph explain how your style is unique compared to another artist of your choice.

MAIN COURSE

Mystery Meat Burger

What is the mystery behind style? Where does it come from? Why do we all have different styles even if we use the same media? Explore the mystery of what can affect artists' styles by completing the Style Mystery entry in your journal. The entry description and resources to help you can be found in the art library.

DESSERT

Try It on Truffle

Choose an artist who has a style that you admire that is different from your own. Try on their style as you create a piece of art. Fill out a proposal sheet that includes the artist, style description, subject of your work, and media choice.

Mixed-Up Berry Pie

Use mixed media to create a portrait of someone you admire. First consider what defines their style and use their style to direct what colors, lines, shapes, and look your piece will have.

Second Time Around Cake

Recreate one of your favorite pieces from your portfolio using a different style, but the same media choice.

6.11 ***Menu Example: The Style It Café.*** **Menus add both choices for students and control over content for teachers.** Created by Heather L. R. Fountain.

written, auditory, or kinesthetic. One of the strengths of this strategy lies in its flexibility and ease of use. You can choose any three categories that you feel are important for your students to consider depending on what key concepts you are teaching. For instance, a Think-Tac-Toe board was used in a unit where students had been considering how artists use color and composition to convey certain emotions. The students were asked to make three choices; each choice had to be in a different category. The Think-Tac-Toe strategy ensured that students did not choose three choices in one category, but rather that they had to demonstrate their proficiency in all three categories. (See the Appendix, sheet A.6.3 for the *Think-Tac-Toe* example.)

STRATEGY

What Does RAFT Differentiate?

The role students choose while using this strategy determines what they will create in response; therefore, this strategy is ideal in differentiating the product of a lesson.

RAFT

RAFT, an acronym for *role, audience, format,* and *topic,* is a strategy that helps students to consider a topic from the point of view of another person.[10] This is very effective as you can use it to help students' think outside of their own experiences and consider a topic from a different perspective.

With this strategy, students take on a role (art critic, parent, artist, and so forth) and create a learning product (for example, book, song, artwork, news report) about a specific topic for a certain audience such as children visiting a museum, the Mona Lisa, your grandmother, etc.

With this strategy, students choose a role and follow the RAFT elements horizontally across the chart to discover what their topic and format will be, and who will serve as their audience. (See sheet A.6.4 in the Appendix for an *Art Criticism RAFT* example.)

TRY THIS

Creating Strong Objectives

To clarify the learning goals of a lesson for yourself and your students, take a moment and consider what you want them to know, understand, and be able to do as a result of their engagement with the lesson's content. When posted in the classroom, this lesson design strategy, called a "KUD," can create a clear and visual understanding of the goals and objectives of a lesson, for yourself and for your students. You can also use it as a tool to help you clarify your own direction while designing a lesson.

Next time you design a lesson, look at the learning standards you want students to meet and consider what you want them to know, understand, and do.

Know:

Understand:

Do:

Choice Boards or Cards

Another strategy for offering students choice in a lesson is a choice board or a set of choice cards. The only difference between choice cards and choice boards are how the choices are displayed. Choice boards consist of choices that are hung on a wall or even a tri-fold display in three columns; whereas choice cards are choices that are placed on a ring, so that students can flip through them. The initial step in either of these tools begins with defining the learning goals for your students—what do you want them to know (K), understand (U), and be able to do (D)? Next, you will need to decide whether you will make choices designed around student learning styles (verbal, written, kinesthetic, or auditory) or by using the eight multiple intelligences areas (verbal/linguistic, mathematical/logical, visual/spatial, bodily/kinesthetic, musical/rhythmical, naturalistic/environmental, interpersonal, and intrapersonal).

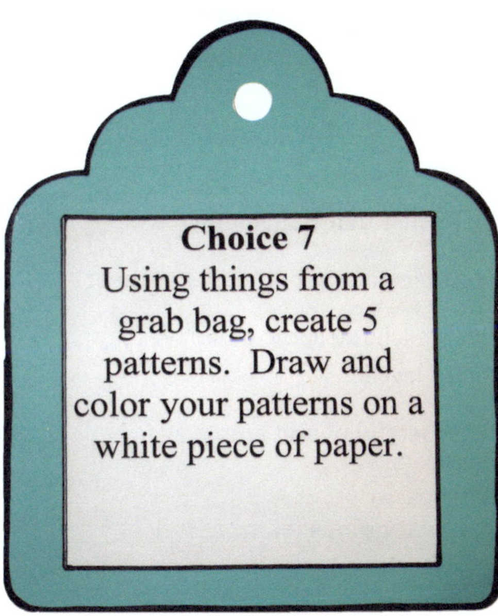

6.12 Choice cards can be designed so that each choice matches a Multiple Intelligences area. This is one of the eight choice cards created by an elementary teacher to help her students explore pattern. Pattern choice card created by and used with the permission of Marcie Khuns.

STRATEGY

What Do Choice Boards or Cards Differentiate?

You can use this strategy to help differentiate the process of how students explore a topic, or you can use it to differentiate the product students create as they demonstrate what they have learned through the lesson or unit.

It is important that all your choices are equally interesting, engaging, and fun for students while also being beneficial in helping them to meet or demonstrate their achievement of the learning goals. If a choice is fun but doesn't help them to meet the learning goal, then it does not meet the criteria for a choice board or cards.

You can use a choice board or a set of choice cards to help students extend their learning about a lesson topic by offering related, rich activities. You can also use these tools to provide students with the chance to investigate another art topic once they have completed their original assignment. Some teachers use choice boards or cards at artist-of-the-month exploration stations. Another idea is to create an artist study center that you could set up in your class for half or all of the school year. Students can work independently on their choices when they have free time. This ensures that students will use all the available time they have in art class to learn about art in productive and exciting ways.

TIPS

Choice Boards

Check your choice board to ensure that it includes:

1 Clearly identified learning objectives for students to meet.

2 Choices that help students reach the same objectives but in varied ways and at varied levels.

3 Choices that are equally respectful of and engaging for all students.

4 Choices that address students' various learning styles and/or multiple intelligences areas.

5 Purposeful guidance that assists students in making choices that help them grow in their learning.

Keep in mind that you can guide the choices that students make by setting parameters or requiring certain choices. For example, you could state that all students must complete a certain choice before moving onto their own choices, or you could require them to choose one option from each column. Parameters such as these will ensure that all students complete choices that challenge them, while still having some autonomy.

continued on next page

Elementary Artist Choice Board

Choice 1	Choice 2	Choice 3
Create a cheer for your favorite artist. Be sure to include why you think this person is the best artist you know. Include their artwork in your presentation.	Create a poem about your favorite artist that details his or her life and work. Set the poem to a familiar song such as "Row, Row, Row Your Boat."	Create a play retelling a story or main event in your favorite artist's life. Make sure that the events are in the correct order.
Choice 4	**Choice 5**	**Choice 6**
Use natural materials to recreate a piece of art in the style of your favorite artist. It can be similar to an existing piece or a copy.	Create an award for your favorite piece of art that your artist created. Give your award a title. Write down the reasons for the award.	Create a timeline of the main events of your artist's life or work in chronological order.
Choice 7	**Choice 8**	**Choice 9**
A famous film studio wants to make a movie about your artist. They want you to create a movie poster that can be hung up in movie theaters around the country to advertise the movie. Design a poster using the most important or exciting events from your artist's life.	Some people like to know more about artists and their work before they decide to research them. Create a cube out of paper. On each side, illustrate aspects of your artist's life and work. Be sure to design it in a way that will be noticed by others and will attract them to your cube.	Create a pop-up picture that shows an important event in your artist's life. Fold a piece of paper in half so it looks like a small book. Design the cover including a title and create a pop-up scene inside.

6.13 *Elementary Artist Study Choice Board.* Used as a center, choice boards provide a place for students to extend learning when they have time between lessons. Created by Heather L. R. Fountain.

continued on next page

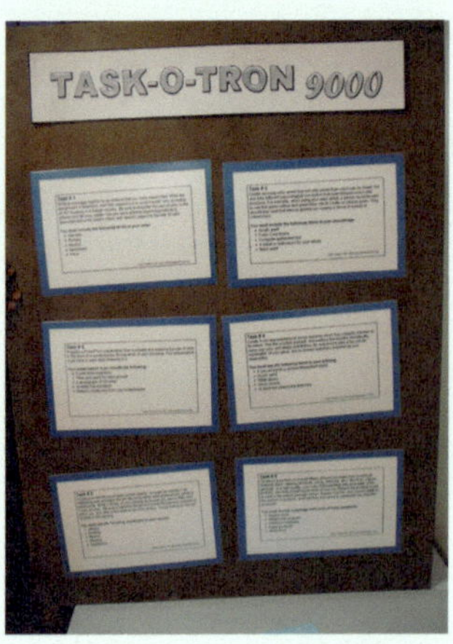

6.14 ***High School Color Theory Choice Board: Task-O-Tron 9000.*** **Choice boards help students meet the same objectives, but provide different ways to accomplish these goals.** Created by and used with permission from Nick Urffer.

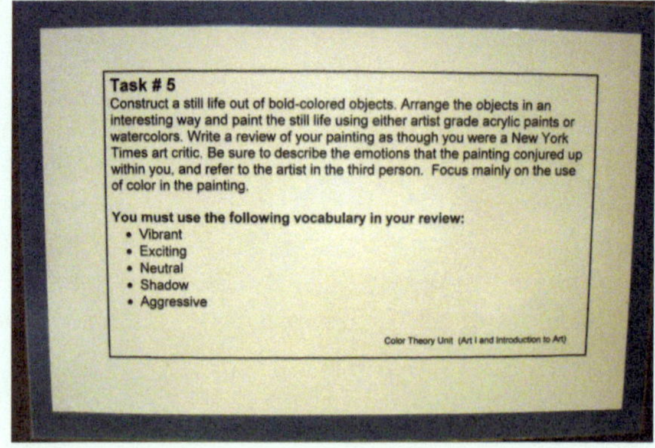

Task # 5
Construct a still life out of bold-colored objects. Arrange the objects in an interesting way and paint the still life using either artist grade acrylic paints or watercolors. Write a review of your painting as though you were a New York Times art critic. Be sure to describe the emotions that the painting conjured up within you, and refer to the artist in the third person. Focus mainly on the use of color in the painting.

You must use the following vocabulary in your review:

- Vibrant
- Exciting
- Neutral
- Shadow
- Aggressive

Color Theory Unit (Art I and Introduction to Art)

6.15 ***Close-up of a choice card from the High School Color Theory Choice Board: Task-O-Tron 9000.*** Created by and used with permission from Nick Urffer.

TRY THIS

Overwhelmed

If you are not sure where to start because you are overwhelmed by all the choices for differentiating instruction, try this tip:

> Take one lesson that you have already taught and apply one of the Differentiated Instruction strategies from this chapter to modify the process or product of your lesson.

Final Considerations

There are so many challenging and effective strategies that you can use in the art classroom. It is important to remember that no matter which strategy you use with your students, they all have the same goal: to help students connect with the knowledge and skills that you deem important for them to learn. To be completely successful in using any of these strategies, it is essential that you have clear learning objectives in place from the start and use them to design choices that help students explore, discover, and share what they have learned in different ways.

REFLECTION & PRACTICE

Designing Instruction

Tiering After pre-assessing your students on a topic, sort their responses into piles depending on their readiness or knowledge about the topic. Count how many students seem to have high levels of knowledge, average levels of knowledge, and low or no knowledge of the topic. This quick count will provide you with a rough idea of what students already know, and will allow you to create tiers of engagement in your lesson, so that all students can successfully meet the objectives without getting bored or overwhelmed. Take an activity, worksheet, or even a product being created and vary that lesson idea so you have three options that help students with lower, average, and higher levels of readiness meet the objectives with success. Take a look at the tiered example in chapter 7 and the tiered setting sheets (A.6.5a–c in the Appendix).

Grouping Consider how to use grouping to your advantage in a lesson. Try pairing students who have different MI strengths or learning styles together in one group. Once you have decided on a task or lesson that calls for grouping, have students explore a station, brainstorm an idea, create artwork, or analyze a piece of artwork together. This strategy will help your students contribute through their unique strengths, and also will help them collectively see things in different ways that they may not have considered if they completed the task alone.

Choice Based Learning Strategies Consider a lesson that you currently teach; how can it be redesigned to include student choice? Use one of the following strategies to provide students with ownership in their learning process: Learning Menu, Think-Tac-Toe, RAFT, Choice Board, or Choice Cards. To help you plan a choice board or choice cards, a *Planning for Differentiation by Multiple Intelligences Preference* sheet can be found in the Appendix (see A.5.7b).

Notes

1 C. A. Tomlinson, *How to Differentiate Instruction in Mixed-Ability Classrooms*, 2nd ed. (Alexandria, VA: Association for Supervision and Curriculum Development, 2001).

2 As quoted in Willis, S. (Nov. 1993) Teaching Young Children. ASCD Curriculum Update Newsletter.

3 C. A. Tomlinson, *The Differentiated Classroom: Responding to the Needs of All Learners* (Alexandria, VA: Association for Supervision and Curriculum Development, 1999).

4 J. Caldwell and M. P. Ford, *Where Have All the Bluebirds Gone? How to Soar with Flexible Grouping.* (Portsmouth, NH: Heinemann, 2002).

5 Y. Lou, P. C. Abrami, J. C. Spence, C. Poulsen, B. Chambers, and S. d' Apollonio, "Within-class Grouping: A Meta-analysis," *Review of Educational Research,* 66(4) (1996): pp. 423-458; H. F. Silver, R. W. Strong, and M. J. Perini, (2000). *So Each May Learn: Integrating Learning Styles and Multiple Intelligences* (Alexandria, VA: Association for Supervision and Curriculum Development, 2000); C. A. Tomlinson, *How to Differentiate Instruction in Mixed-Ability Classrooms,* 2nd ed. (Alexandria, VA: Association for Supervision and Curriculum Development, 2001); R. Wormeli, *Differentiation: From Planning to Practice, Grades 6–12* (Portland, ME: Stenhouse Publications, 2007).

6 Howard Gardner, *The Unschooled Mind: How Children Think and How Schools Should Teach* (New York: Basic Books, 1991).

7 L. Anderson and L. Sosniak, eds., *Bloom's Taxonomy of Educational Objectives: A Forty-Year Retrospective* (Chicago: The University of Chicago Press, 1994); B. S. Bloom (1984). *Taxonomy of Educational Objectives, Book I: The Cognitive Domain (2nd Ed.).* (New York: Addison Wesley Publishing Company).

8 ThinkDots were created in 1999 by Kay Brimijoin. You can find examples and further information in C. A. Tomlinson, *Fulfilling the Promise of a Differentiated Classroom: Strategies and Tools for Responsive Teaching* (Alexandria, VA: Association for Supervision and Curriculum Development, 2003).

9 E. Aronson, N. Blaney, C. Stephan, J. Sikes, and M. Snapp, *The Jigsaw Classroom* (Beverly Hills, CA: Sage Publications, Inc., 1978).

10 D. Buehl, *Classroom Strategies for Interactive Learning* (Portsmouth, NH: Heinemann, 2001).

Chapter 7

Differentiated Lesson Examples

"It's teaching so that 'typical' students, students with disabilities, students who are gifted, and students with a range of cultural, ethnic, and language groups can learn together, well.

Not inclusion, but inclusive teaching."

J. M. Peterson and M. M. Hittie[1]

CONSIDER THIS

Here are a few things that one teacher had to say after a year of implementing DI in her classroom:

"I feel that I have reached more students, [which has made them] more successful and [they] have enjoyed the year more . . . and done so in a way that fits many of their learning styles. It [the classroom] has become a more pleasant place to work and come to every day.

". . . students who [haven't been] as involved as they could be were much more involved . . . and did much better [with the concepts] than they had in the past. There was a lot more involvement from all of the students."

Karen, Elementary Teacher

Differentiated Instruction in Action

Sometimes having a visual representation of an idea is the best way to begin understanding how all its pieces fit together. When I first began differentiating in my classroom, there were no examples of differentiated art lessons available, and I couldn't find another art teacher who had started to use Differentiated Instruction.

What I did find was a PBS series called *The Eddie Files* about a teacher named Kay Toliver.[2] This woman was humorous and inspirational, but most importantly, she showed me what her classroom, her students, and her lessons looked like when she focused on her students' needs and built engaging lessons that considered all students. She and her students dressed up, danced, read poetry, made fraction pizzas, and sang—whatever it took to engage her students in learning. Even though the series was not a glimpse into an art classroom, Kay Toliver helped me truly begin to understand how to make learning fun, engaging, and centered on students' needs by teaching in various ways that helped them connect to learning.

Through the years, I looked for examples of how teachers were using Differentiated Instruction in art classrooms, but continued to find nothing. This chapter will provide you with what I could not find for myself: examples of differentiated lessons at the elementary, middle, and high school levels, so you can see how to make DI a reality in your own art classroom.

PERSONAL CONNECTIONS

Planning for Success

As you read, consider the following questions:

1 Am I an inclusive teacher?

2 Are there types of students that I pay more or less attention to than others? Why is that?

3 What specific needs do the students in my school community have?

Elementary: Keep It Real—Grade 2

At the start of a school year, I asked my second grade students to think of and list the three things they most wanted to learn in art that year. In their table groups, students had five minutes to decide what their top-three choices would be and I wrote the results on the board. As expected, using clay was the top choice mentioned by every group in every second grade class. The other top choices that were repeated multiple times by class groups were: drawing things in a way that made them look real and how to draw animals.

At first, I was shocked at this result, as students of this age often don't consider drawing realistically until they get a bit older. I was unsure of what students already knew, except that they had learned about the concept of realistic versus abstract in first grade. I created a pre-assessment drawing activity to help me gauge each student's concept of realistic drawing and to assess their motor-skill development. This quick pre-assessment enabled me to see how students' knowledge, skills, and physical abilities varied so that I could design my lesson accordingly and with appropriate challenges through the use of tiering, grouping, or other adaptations to media and tasks.

A lesson in realism unfolded in the following way: On the first day of this lesson, students entered the room and all the lights were off except one floor lamp. I had placed the floor lamp so that it became a spotlight shining on a small, white still life that was placed on white paper in the front of the classroom. I asked the students to look at the still life and tell me what they saw. Initially, they listed the items in the still life, and then one boy noted that the still-life objects were "so bright" on the side closest to the light. This led to others noting that it was dark on the side away from the light and dark on the white paper underneath or next to the items in the still life.

I asked for a volunteer and had her turn to face the chalkboard while I moved the light to shine on her back. I asked two questions: Does anyone see a shadow and, if so, where? What is a shadow? Students volunteered many answers and decided that a shadow is a dark place that is "kind of" the shape of the thing that makes it. They also observed that "having no light" makes a shadow. They noticed that shadows can be under things and on things, because our volunteer was "shadowed" on the side of her body without the light and that a shadow was on the floor, starting under her feet.

I moved the light back to the still life to see if we could find shadows on things and under things. I had a student walk up and trace the outline of the shadow she saw on the white paper beneath the still life and shade it in with the pencil to help us all see where the shadow was located and what shape it made under the object. I challenged students to walk to their tables and take a look at the still lifes they found on them and see if they could draw the shapes and add in the shadows they saw. At each table was a still life of solid white Styrofoam shapes on white paper. I wanted to help students focus on the shapes and shadows and not be distracted by patterns or colors.

Throughout class, students worked on drawing their still-life objects while thinking about size, shape, shadows, and overlapping. About five minutes before clean-up time, I informed students that they could add any details to their pictures that would help make them look more realistic. Some added darker shadows, others added dots to help describe the texture on the shapes.

As they turned in their drawings at the end of class, I quickly noted a wide range of motor-skill development, as well as the varying degrees of acuity with which students recorded the three-dimensional qualities of the items in the still lifes. Using these two criteria, I sorted their images into piles that I used to help me form groups based on student readiness.

The next step I considered was how to match my students with an appropriate challenge that would help push them to reach higher levels of achievement without over-challenging them. Using the objects I had available, I set up five still-life subjects which students could choose to draw: a raccoon on a log, a pheasant on a rock, a trailing plant in a pot, a cactus in an unusual planter, and a box of sea shells from which students could choose one shell. I assigned students to their groups by placing at each table a presorted pile of drawings they had

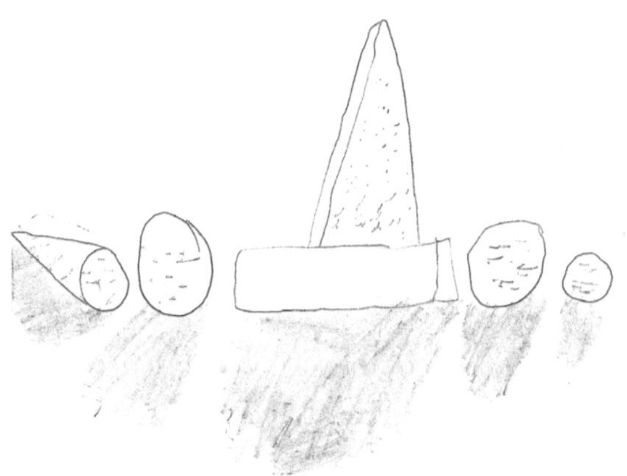

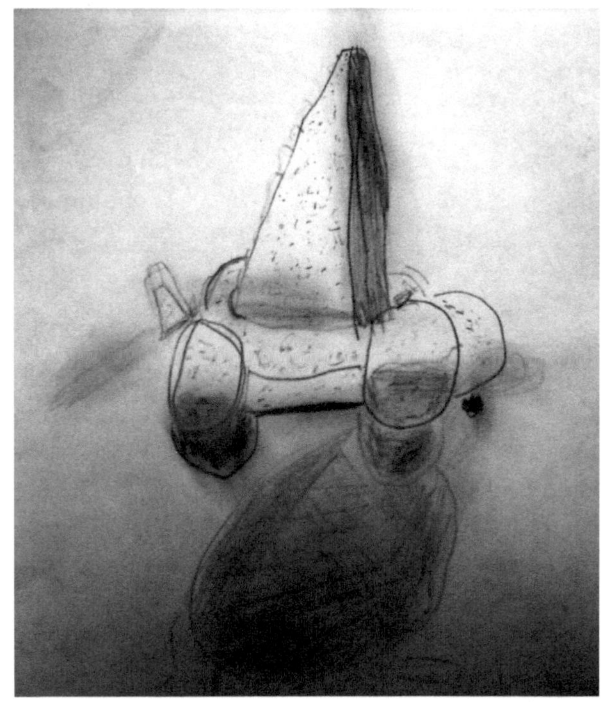

7.1 and 7.2 Students' still-life drawings were used as a pre-assessment to gauge the level of challenge they were ready to take on. Photo by H. L. R. Fountain.

previously completed. A student helper from the preceding class spread the drawings around each table so that students could easily identify their artwork and find their assigned group for the day.

The regular routine for second grade was to enter the classroom and head straight for the meeting area, a rocking chair and a rug in the corner of my room, for directions, stories, or other news. Once on the rug, we would wait for everyone to be ready—hands to ourselves, eyes ready to learn, ears open, and lips zipped. First, I asked students to recall what we had done in our last class and what we had been trying to figure out. They shared various answers that helped them collectively remember things such as: "Still lifes are still, not moved around or you mess up someone's picture. Shadows are dark! Shadows can be on things or under things. Sometimes shapes are funny. Shadows can be shapes."

Next, I asked students what they noticed that was different about our room today. They quickly spotted the raccoon and pheasant followed by the other still-life items. As they chattered about what they wanted to draw, I gave them a challenge: "Your first challenge today, once I give you your piece of paper, is to find your picture from last class on a table and sit at that table for today. I chose your first still-life challenge for today, but in another class, you will have the opportunity to choose your own second challenge." This helped limit the number of complaints about wanting to draw something at another table.

For two class periods, students worked on the still lifes I had chosen for them. During each class, I made them pause once during work time to introduce another element to their still lifes that could help their pictures look more realistic. On day one, we touched textured items and looked at textured pictures

TRY THIS

Creating Art—Students with Visual Impairments

- Provide art materials with textures such as papers, cloth, ribbons, yarn, sandpaper, sand, rice, dried peas, or beans.
- Work on art pieces that use three dimensions instead of two.
- Create high contrast so things are easily seen such as white or yellow on black.
- Use small objects to create mosaics, collages, or mixed-media paintings.
- Mix black paint with white all-purpose glue and place it in a glue bottle. Students can use this to create lines on a paper or canvas that, when dried, will have a raised texture. You can use this same tool to help watercolor paint stay contained within defined areas. Students can also use white glue to create raised lines on images or artwork that they can feel, but the lines will be less visible than the black glue lines.
- Add textures to paint, such as sand in the yellow, to help distinguish the colors from one another. Many common household items such as cornmeal, rice, quinoa, glitter, salt or even shaving cream can be use to create various textures.
- Use cooking extracts to add small amounts of scent to paints. This will help students distinguish one color from another. For example, add a drop of peppermint extract to blue, cinnamon to red, orange to orange, lemon to yellow, vanilla to white, lime to green, and licorice to black.
- Consistently place art media in the same location. For instance, paint on a palette could always be in rainbow order. This will allow the student to feel the order of the paints and know the placement of the colors. Even though they may not be able to see the color, they should be able to make choices.

to identify the textures; together, they advised me of how to draw those textures with pencil, which I did on large paper so that it was visible to all. I also shared a few techniques they had not figured out on their own. This helped students to see, hear, touch, and connect with a variety of textures on a sensory level. On day two, I showed students two drawings of the same rabbit, one with details, texture, and shading; and one drawn with a contour line with a shadow under it. I asked them which rabbit looked more realistic and why. They liked the rabbit with details, texture, and shading.

Next, we considered details. We discussed what they are and how we find them. Students noted that details were "things on things" like patterns, hair, textures, eyes, eyelashes, and so forth. I challenged them to go back to their own drawings and see if there were any details they could add to make them look more realistic.

Grouping students by appropriate levels of challenge helped all of them to accomplish amazingly realistic finished pieces without finding the task too difficult or too frustrating. Students who finished their first challenge could choose an item from a mystery bag, find an empty seat at another still-life station, or choose a shell from the shell box to draw. This extension activity accomplished three goals:

1. It provided a meaningful way for students to apply and practice their drawing skills.
2. It gave students a chance to choose their own item to draw.
3. It served as good classroom management for those who finished sooner than their peers.

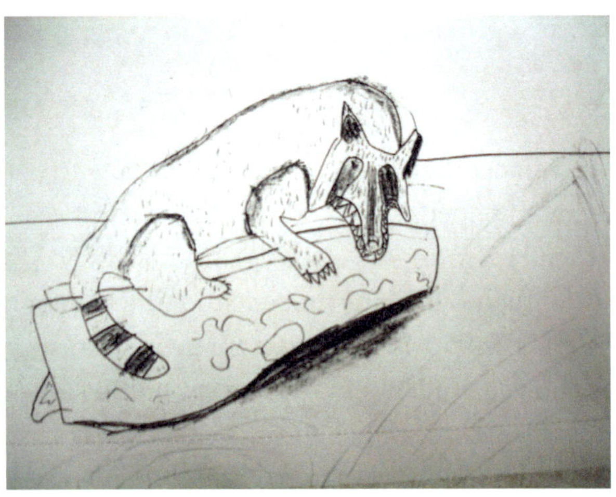

7.3 At table 1, students sketched a still life of a raccoon on a log. Photo by Heather L. R. Fountain.

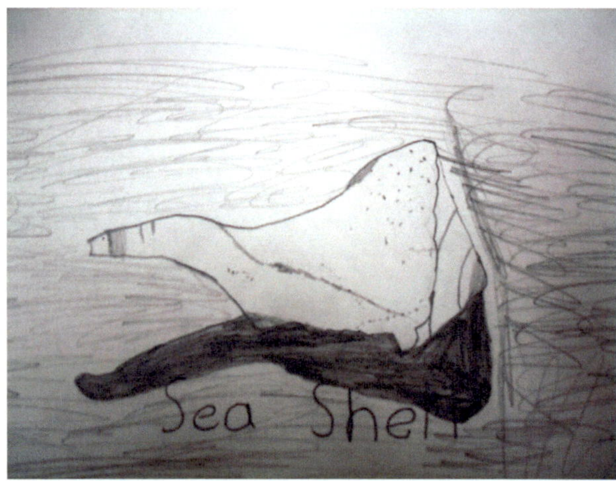

7.4 At table 2, a shell was the subject students sketched for their still lifes. Photo by Heather L. R. Fountain.

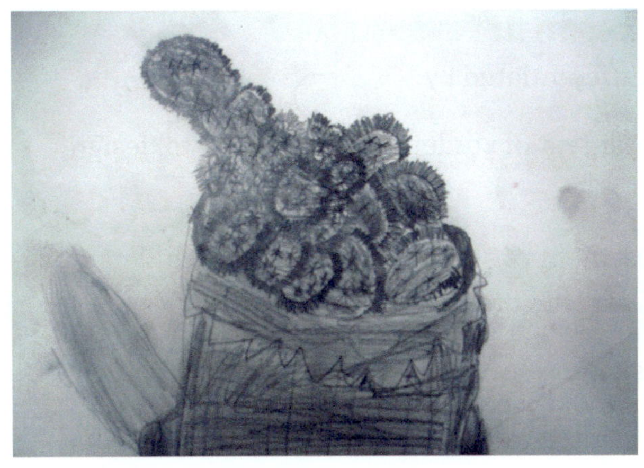

7.5 At table 3, a cactus provided students with a variety of textures to include in their drawings. Photo by Heather L. R. Fountain.

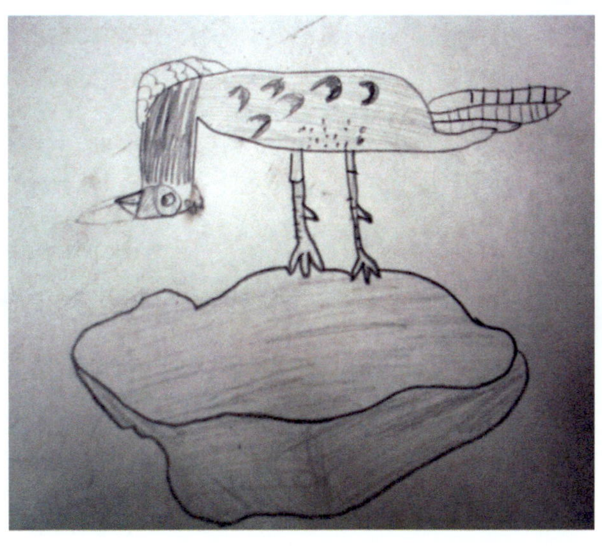

7.6 At table 4, a pheasant on a rock was the subject for students' still lifes. Photo by Heather L. R. Fountain.

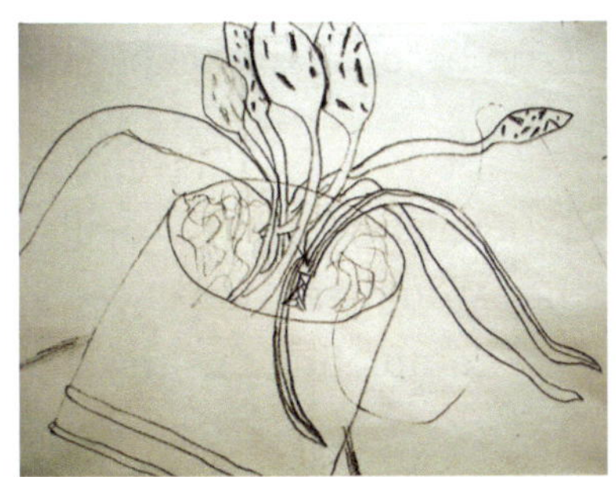

7.7 At table 5, students sketched a still life of a leafy plant. Photo by Heather L. R. Fountain.

It amazed me how students of such a young age were able to accomplish so much in their artwork through the use of tiering. This strategy helped give students confidence and enabled them to tackle a new and seemingly difficult task. At the end of this lesson, students were amazed at how realistic their drawings were and they impressed me and their parents with their accomplishments.

What was differentiated in this lesson?

Tiering differentiated the content of this lesson by providing various levels of difficulty that matched students' needs based on their motor-skill development and their knowledge of realistic drawing. Students' choices for their own second challenge differentiated the product, if they finished early and had time to create a second drawing.

How was the lesson differentiated?

This lesson was differentiated by:

- Using pre-assessment of students' art interests to design a lesson.
- Using pre-assessment of students' readiness to understand the concept of realistic drawing.
- Pre-assessing students' levels of motor-skill development.
- Using pre-assessment information to design a lesson that was tiered, creating five levels of challenge.
- Providing students with a choice for their second drawing.

Why was it differentiated?

This lesson was differentiated so that students would:

- Have greater investment in the lesson because they chose its topic.
- Be invested in the project because they would gain the skills they had requested and because they would earn a free choice for the second challenge after completing the first challenge.
- Be able to work on the same key concepts and skills at levels that were appropriately challenging and not too overwhelming.

Middle School: Freedom—What Does It Really Mean?

After overhearing a student make a flippant comment about how "it's a free country so I can do whatever I want," a colleague and I started to think about how to help students seriously consider the concept of freedom. Students in middle school learn about issues and events historically related to freedom such as slavery, the Holocaust, and civil rights. They also gain the ability to think about and discuss complex issues. Combine that with their desire to have more freedom in their own lives and it seemed like freedom could be an enduring theme that would connect with students in personal ways. This led me to design an art lesson that would help students to consider freedom from many perspectives, including both its costs and benefits.

My first step was to determine what students should know, understand, and be able to do as a result of the lesson (see the sidebar Try This: Creating Strong Objectives in chapter 6 on p. 141). The KUD lesson objectives I identified were:

Know

- Students will consider what freedom means and write a definition in their journal to use as an initial prompt for exploring the topic.
- In small groups, students will compare and contrast their ideas and points of view on the qualities that define freedom to help them understand that people can have different views on an idea.

Understand

- Student will respectfully discuss and express their ideas about the topic.
- Through the completion of three reflection activities, students will consider the concept of freedom—its costs, risks, and benefits.

- Students will revisit their original definition and revise it or add to it, as necessary, in closing reflection.
- Students will use art media appropriately, with safety and care, to show their respect for the art classroom, their peers, and themselves.

Do

- Students will fully complete three or more choice board options, following the specific directions for each, to help them explore the concept of freedom through various art modes: production, aesthetics, criticism, and history.
- Students will fill out a choice board contract with at least three choices and their reasons for those choices.
- Student will use media to create a visual statement that not only expresses their ideas about an issue related to freedom, but also explores how artists communicate visually.

I was unsure of how deeply students understood the concept of freedom or if they had ever considered it as a topic related to art, so I created a pre-assessment think sheet to see what their initial ideas about freedom would be and to get them thinking about it. (See sheet A.7.1 in the Appendix for the *Freedom* think sheet.)

As students entered the room on the first day of this lesson, each received a *Let Freedom Ring* card (see sheet A.7.2 in the Appendix for examples)[3] that had one fact related to some aspect of freedom. Students read their card and, using it as a prompt, took a few minutes to write at least three sentences in their journals that reflected on how the fact related to freedom.

Next, they circulated around the room to find others with the same card. In small groups of two or three, they discussed their thoughts about that particular fact and how it relates to the idea of freedom. Each group shared their fact with the whole class as well as one of the ideas they had discussed in their groups. At the end of this class, students had a few minutes to add to or reconsider their original journal entry on the definition of freedom and its costs or benefits. They also listed four freedoms that they have in their lives.

On the second day of class, once students had entered the room and retrieved their journals, I asked them to raise their hands in response to two questions:

1 How many of you would like more freedom in your life?

2 How many of you would like more chances to make decisions about your life and about what you learn?

I informed students that, in the spirit of freedom, they would have the opportunity to choose what projects they would like to complete in a new lesson that explores the idea of freedom. I also let them know that with the freedom to choose a project comes the responsibility to set action plans to help them accomplish their goals and not fall behind or off task. At that point, I gave students two items: a copy of the Freedom Choice Board for their journals and a Freedom Choice Board Contract to complete. (See the sheets A.7.3 in the Appendix for a *Freedom Choice Board* example and A.7.4 for a *Freedom Choice Board Contract* example.)

In preparation, I placed multiple copies of any additional necessary materials in numbered folders that corresponded to the nine different choice board options. I placed these folders at the choice board display, so students could easily find the items they needed, such as graphic organizers, articles, or directions that identified standards of completion to guide them in completing their assignments (see sheet A.7.5 in the Appendix for an example of Choice 1 additional materials). In addition to students exploring artworks in a variety of ways, I wanted to be sure they all created a piece of artwork, so I included some choice stipulations in their contracts.

The final step of this lesson asked students to return to their original definitions of freedom, its costs, and its benefits, and add or change any information they thought necessary. The words of one student summarized the growth in perspective of many other students: "Freedom is expensive! It can even cost your life sometimes, so you have to be really careful to use it wisely."

What was differentiated in this lesson?

The process of this lesson was differentiated as students used various activities and modes of communication to engage in the enduring idea of freedom. The product of this lesson was also differentiated as students created a variety of works that demonstrated their competency and grasp of the enduring idea of freedom.

How was the lesson differentiated?

The process in this lesson was differentiated through the use of a choice board that allowed students to explore the concept of freedom in various ways that would be attractive to all multiple intelligences preferences, but would also challenge students to work in areas that needed strengthening by identifying certain requirements.

TRY THIS

Middle School Logos

Differentiate a lesson on logos by creating three different challenges for your students. Each challenge will have the same goal—to help students think about and recall logos in different ways—but will require them to use different learning strengths to complete the challenge.

- Challenge 1: *What can you remember?*
  Your challenge is to draw as many logos as you can remember. Think about the lines, shapes, and colors used.
- Challenge 2: *The perfect pair.*
  Your challenge is to match the following slogans with the logos of the companies they represent. 1. Have it your way. 2. Food, folks, fun! 3. I'm lovin' it! 4. Nothing runs like a Deere. 5. We bring good things to life. 6. Just do it! 7. Think outside the bun. (You can either choose a slogan and have students draw its matching logo, or you can have a list of slogans and a list of logos that students connect by drawing a line between them.)
- Challenge 3: *Find me if you can.*
  Your challenge is to search through magazines and newspapers to find as many logos as you can. See how many you can find and add to your paper before time runs out! (You can either have students sketch the logos or cut and paste them on their paper.)

What is differentiated in this lesson?

You can differentiate the process of how students interact and explore the concept of logos by creating three different ways for them to engage in learning.

Why is this lesson differentiated?

Each challenge is designed with a different learning style in mind. Three options will engage more students in ways that allow them to use their strengths by tapping into their individual learning styles. Challenge 1 helps visual/spatial learners recall images they have seen and focus on recreating them. Challenge 2 provides written clues that help logical/mathematical learners identify the pairs, offers written information for verbal/linguistic students, and even taps into musical/rhythmical intelligence through the recall of jingles. Challenge 3 is designed for students with both bodily/kinesthetic and naturalistic/environmental intelligences. This challenge allows students to move around the room (bodily/kinesthetic) searching for items.

Why was it differentiated?

The process in this lesson was differentiated to provide students:

- Choice in their learning, which lead to higher levels of motivation and pride in their work.
- Various ways to engage in and process the enduring idea of freedom.

High School: Clay Pod Memory Vessel

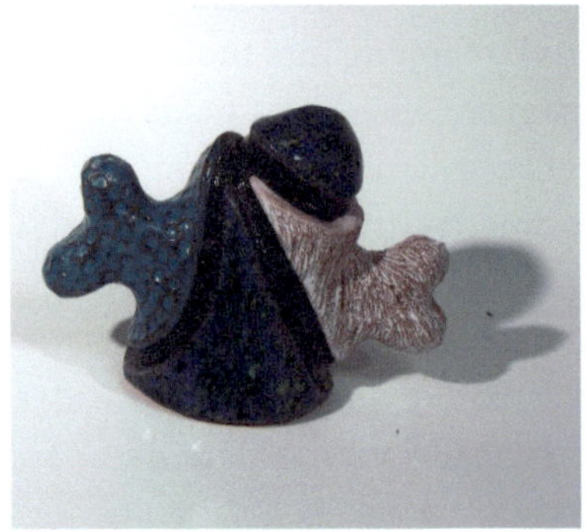

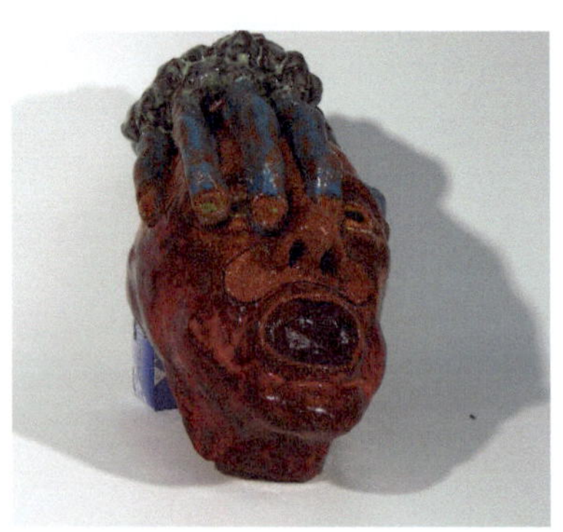

7.8 and 7.9 *Clay pods.* Personal connections to people, memories, or events can build investment in learning and artwork.
Photos by Addy McKerns.

How do you teach clay techniques in a way that helps students connect with the project and value what they have learned? This was the question that led teacher Addy McKerns to consider using DI to modify her existing clay pod lesson. She knew that she wanted students to learn how to create a hollow form using two pinch pots and to learn techniques such as slip, score, and coil to combine the pots. She also wanted students to learn how to attach items to their work and add textures. Inspired by her own personal life, she decided to create a pod in memory of someone she loved and share it with her students. This became the first step in rethinking her clay pod lesson.

Using a laptop cart, McKerns had her students take an online written multiple intelligences test so she could use the information to form teams made up of students with different strengths. The first day of class set the stage for the entire lesson by introducing or reviewing the ideas and concepts that would follow and by gathering pre-assessment information using two tools: the MI pre-test and a self-designed KWL chart. Before the end of class, she introduced students to the three choices they could make about the type of pod they would create: a pod that honored someone, a pod that represented a sacred object, or a pod that symbolized a secret. She also gave them a "Student Information Sheet" that they were directed to put in their art binders. The sheet outlined the purpose of the project, the initial steps involved, and students' responsibilities.

STRATEGY

Using Student Information Sheets

Introduce the Project:
The main purpose of this project is to create a well-designed clay pod using the techniques shown in class, and to create a piece of art that you are proud of and see as something sacred to you. Everyone is required to create two well-formed, balanced, lightweight pinch pots. You will learn how to connect them properly and create a hand-thrown base for better stability. I want you to understand the similarities and differences between visual and tactile texture and pattern.

Step 1 Please fill out one KWL sheet and turn it in at the end of the project.

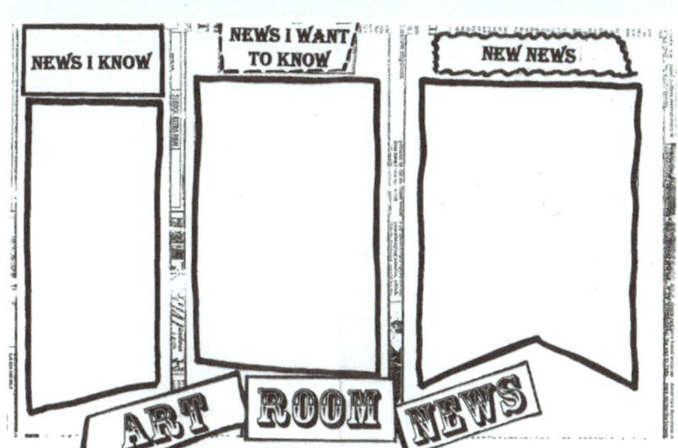

7.10 ***KWL Art Room News.*** **Thinking of new ways to recreate common graphic organizers can add interest and fun to these strategies.** Created by Addy McKerns.

Step 2 Pick up and read the Clay Pod information sheet and the Texture information sheet. I want you to understand how to create pinch pots and texture.

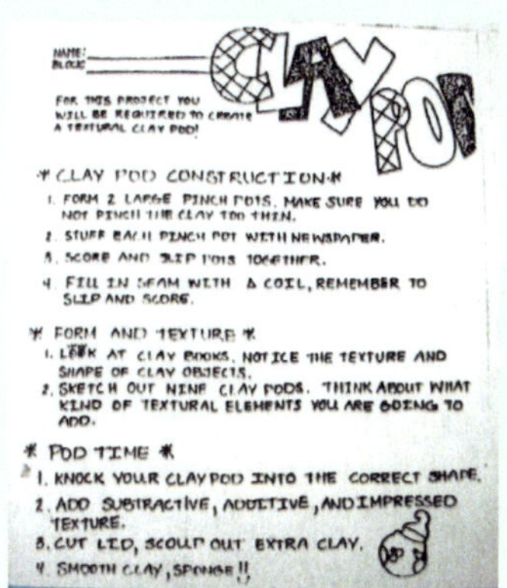

NAME:
BLOCK:

CLAY POD

FOR THIS PROJECT YOU WILL BE REQUIRED TO CREATE A TEXTURAL CLAY POD!

* CLAY POD CONSTRUCTION *
1. FORM 2 LARGE PINCH POTS. MAKE SURE YOU DO NOT PINCH THE CLAY TOO THIN.
2. STUFF EACH PINCH POT WITH NEWSPAPER.
3. SCORE AND SLIP POTS TOGETHER.
4. FILL IN SEAM WITH A COIL, REMEMBER TO SLIP AND SCORE.

* FORM AND TEXTURE *
1. LOOK AT CLAY BOOKS. NOTICE THE TEXTURE AND SHAPE OF CLAY OBJECTS.
2. SKETCH OUT NINE CLAY PODS. THINK ABOUT WHAT KIND OF TEXTURAL ELEMENTS YOU ARE GOING TO ADD.

* POD TIME *
1. KNOCK YOUR CLAY POD INTO THE CORRECT SHAPE.
2. ADD SUBTRACTIVE, ADDITIVE, AND IMPRESSED TEXTURE.
3. CUT LID, SCOOP OUT EXTRA CLAY.
4. SMOOTH CLAY, SPONGE!!

7.11 ***Clay Pod Information Sheet.*** **Providing a sheet with steps helps students know what is expected and serves as a reminder of the project's goals.** Created by Addy McKerns.

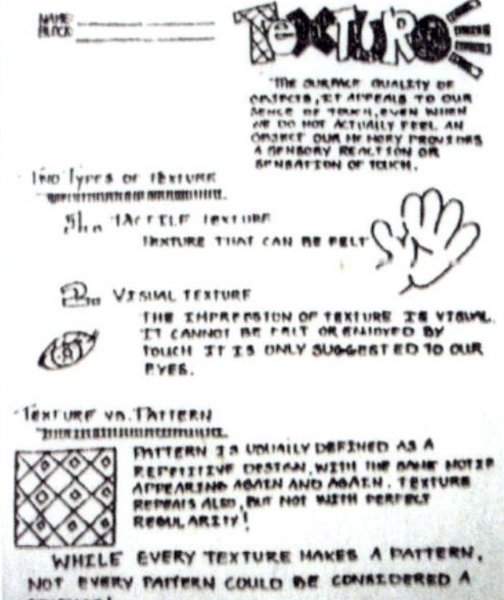

NAME:
BLOCK:

TEXTURE

"THE SURFACE QUALITY OF OBJECTS, IT APPEALS TO OUR SENSE OF TOUCH, EVEN WHEN WE DO NOT ACTUALLY FEEL AN OBJECT OUR MEMORY PROVIDES A SENSORY REACTION OR SENSATION OF TOUCH.

TWO TYPES OF TEXTURE

TACTILE TEXTURE
TEXTURE THAT CAN BE FELT

VISUAL TEXTURE
THE IMPRESSION OF TEXTURE IS VISUAL. IT CANNOT BE FELT OR ENJOYED BY TOUCH IT IS ONLY SUGGESTED TO OUR EYES.

TEXTURE VS. PATTERN
PATTERN IS USUALLY DEFINED AS A REPETITIVE DESIGN, WITH THE SAME MOTIF APPEARING AGAIN AND AGAIN. TEXTURE REPEATS ALSO, BUT NOT WITH PERFECT REGULARITY!

WHILE EVERY TEXTURE MAKES A PATTERN, NOT EVERY PATTERN COULD BE CONSIDERED A TEXTURE!

7.12 ***Texture Information Sheet.*** **When students realize that their teacher made something for them, even an informational sheet, their interest and investment in learning increases.** Created by Addy McKerns.

continued on next page

Step 3 Pick up and complete three handouts from the following folders: Texture Brainstorming, Things to Remember, and Joining Pinch Pots.

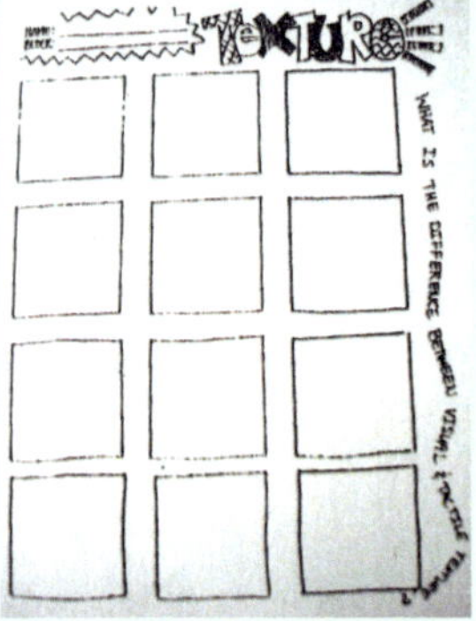

7.13 *Texture Brainstorming Sheet.* Providing students with a place to gather many ideas, even experimental ones, helps them extend their thinking beyond obvious or clichéd answers. Created by Addy McKerns.

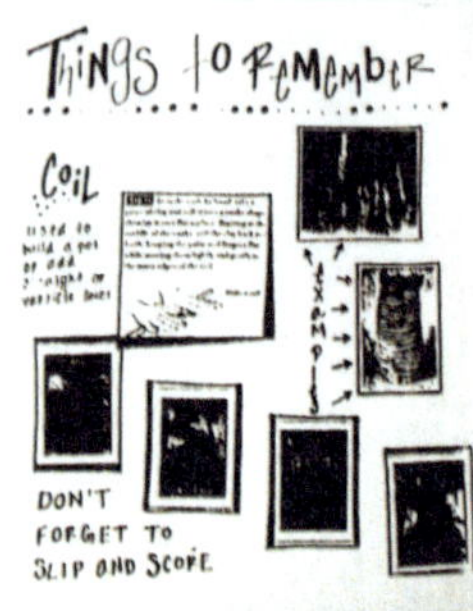

7.14 *Things to Remember Sheet.* Even the most experienced artist needs reminders. Informational sheets help students with ADD/ADHD, those with short memories, or even those who missed class find the tips they need to be successful without fear of looking silly in front of their peers. Created by Addy McKerns.

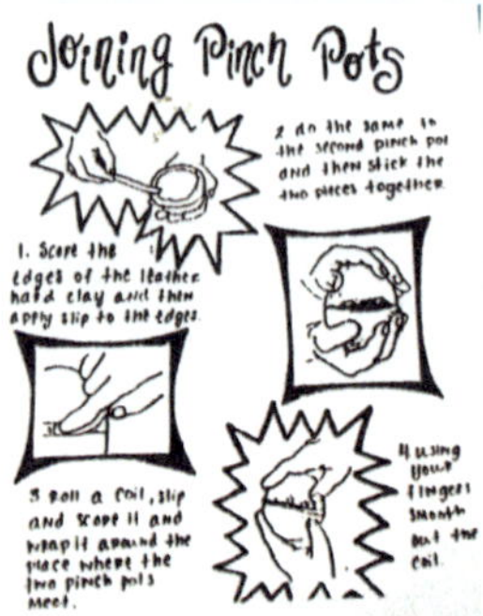

7.15 *Joining Pinch Pots Sheet.* Created by Addy McKerns.

Step 4 Read the **Requirement Sheet.**

Everyone must include all of the following components for the clay project:

a Start with two pinch pots, stuff them with newspaper, and attach them with scoring, slip, and coil. Include a platform or base for the pod and/or feet on the bottom of the pod.

b Include three elements of design on the outside of the pod and/or the base.

c The elements chosen should relate specifically to a person you are honoring, a sacred object, or a secret.

d Include at least three textural elements.

e After you glaze and fire your piece, you must totally complete your project before handing it in.

f You must include in your project book/journal a written reflection on your piece in at least three paragraphs, including your thoughts about any difficulties, challenges, exciting moments, and successes you experienced throughout the process. Most importantly, include your reasons for where you will put your piece when you take it home, or to whom you will give it and why.

When students arrived for the next class, McKerns had used the MI test information to form teams of four students, each of whom had a different MI strength. Her purpose for grouping students with different strengths was to ensure that at least one student would feel really competent at each station and act as a leader so that if a student struggled at a particular task, another member of the group could shine, helping the team complete all tasks successfully. Together, the group would create a whole, each student picking up where other team members felt less confident, reinforcing the idea that all individuals are important and have value. Each team worked to complete six tasks at stations throughout the room for the class period. As the groups moved through the stations, McKerns noticed that the individual members learned so much from each other as they worked together that there was less frustration in completing tasks than if they had worked on their own.

The stations that teams rotated through were:

Activity #1: Elements and Principles

Students looked at information on the elements and principles of art. In their project books, they created small square examples of each element. As a group, they discussed whether they could include all the elements and principles in one 4 x 4" square, which they ultimately attempted in their project books.

Activity #2: Inspiration

Using the class library of magazines, ceramics books, and art images, students looked for patterns, textures, and other elements for inspiration. Students documented at least six items that inspired them and drew 2 x 2" samples, noting the names of the artists who created the works that inspired them,

TRY THIS

Images for Students with Visual Impairments

One of the most difficult challenges for an art teacher is to find ways to adapt lessons to help students with visual impairments understand visual images. Most students who are legally blind have some vision and can see shapes, fields of light and shadow, or even images or words if they are large enough or close enough. Here are a few tips that will help you differentiate classroom instruction to meet the needs of students with visual impairments:

- Provide the student with an individual copy of the image that you are sharing with the whole class. This will allow the student to move or place the image into his or her range of vision as needed.
- Choose an artwork that is sculptural or textured, so that the student can feel it as well as look at it.
- Stand away from windows, so that any glare coming through the window does not further compromise the student's ability to see you or the image you might be sharing with the class.
- When showing an image, provide a visual description of it by using highly descriptive language to explain the details, size, color, and placement of objects within the image.
- Instead of sharing images digitally, provide each table or group with copies of them, so that students can look at them closely and consider them in a more personal way.

as well as the titles and page numbers of the publications in which they had found the elements as a way to help them remember the ideas for future reference.

Activity #3: Fight for What You Believe— This Could Get Loud—It's OK!

McKerns placed ten mugs of various sizes, shapes, colors, and production types in a line on a table. As a team, she directed the students to look at *everything* about the mugs—color, shape, manufacture, design, weight, etc.—and place the mugs in order of value from the highest value, one, through the lowest value, ten. The definition of value was left up to the students' interpretation and therefore led students to categorize the mugs by artistic value, monetary value, or even emotional value—thinking about what their teacher would value most. Then, team members discussed why they each thought different mugs had more or less value than others until they had a final arrangement on which they could all agree. The last steps were to create sketches in their project books of the ten mugs in order of their value and write entries about how they chose the most valued and least valued mugs and why.

TRY THIS

Clay Lesson for Students with Tactile Defensiveness

If you have students who have issues related to tactile sensitivity or defensiveness that cause them to avoid using clay, differentiate the lesson by providing one of the following adaptations:

- Substitute traditional clay with a soft, easy-to-use modeling material or a polymer-based clay.
- Place the clay in a zip-top plastic bag that has enough space to allow the student to model the clay while it stays contained in the bag.
- Provide the student with gloves to wear during the lesson.

Activity #4: Play with Clay

This was an experimental station where each student selected one slab of clay and experimented with the tools available to create line, rhythm, pattern, balance, texture, and emphasis. McKerns encouraged them to add or carve away clay and press items into the slab to create design elements. The final step was to use a rolling pin to flatten the slab into a tile and place the tile on a canvas-covered table.

Activity #5: Ceramic Artists

As a group, students took time to visit websites chosen by McKerns and watch selected videos so they could experience the work of five new ceramic artists. This helped students gather new ideas and inspiration from artists and their work to place in their journals.

Activity #6: Take Time to Choose—Break Away from Your Group

Students looked at the three choices for creating their clay pods:

1 Honor Someone
Choose one person in your life, past or present, whom you hold close to you. Think about someone who has given you hope, love, happiness, and strength. Think of someone you look up to, someone who makes you a better person, or

someone who gives you unconditional love but might not know how important he or she is to you. After choosing the person you want to honor, write down everything you can remember about that person: physical traits, emotions that make you think of that person, things he or she has said, what he or she likes, and anything else that reminds you of this special individual. List why the person is important to you. Then choose three items that best represent the person and write them down. Use words instead of images here.

2 Hold a Sacred Object
List all the physical objects that you have that you could never replace. Circle the one that is most important to you. Where is the item right now? Describe it to me without telling me what it is. Write down the story of why the object is so special to you, when you received it, how long you have had it, if you have ever lost it, and so on. Finally, draw the object using what you know about the elements and principles of art.

3 Represent a Secret—What I Need to Say
This is a personal document and at no time do you have to show it to anyone. You may use this worksheet as a guide to help you share a secret or get something else off your mind. Make sure you glue it into your project book so that I know which project you have chosen. You will place your actual written document in the clay pod right before firing to ensure privacy. Please use the space provided on this think sheet to write your thoughts. What do you need to get off your mind? You can write whatever you are feeling or thinking—anything goes. No one is ever going to read it. Think about why your message is so private and investigate, through self-discovery, why it must or must not remain that way. This project might be a way for you to open up about issues that affect you every day.

TRY THIS

High School Portraits

Lessons that help students create art through building personal connections can greatly increase their levels of commitment and motivation. During a lesson on portraits, give students three options to help them explore portraits in ways that build upon those personal connections. Be sure that your objectives are clearly stated from the beginning so that all students, no matter what option they choose, know the standards they must attain.

Option 1 Interview a senior member of your community. Find out who he or she is beyond what is instantly visible. Consider asking the following questions: What is your greatest accomplishment? What interests or hobbies do you have? What words would you use to describe yourself? Use the information you gather to create a portrait of the person that helps to capture what you learn through your interview process. Once completed, you will photograph the portrait for your portfolio and present the artwork to the person you interviewed.

Option 2 Research an artist, living or dead, whom you admire for something great that they have accomplished. Use your research to discover information about the artist, his or her artwork, and how he or she learned his or her craft. Next, create a portrait of this person that displays aspects of what you have discovered through your research.

Option 3 Compile a collection of fifteen or more photographs of a person to whom you are close. Use at least one detail from each photograph to help you create a composite portrait of the person. Be sure to consider carefully what context the details you place around the person will provide to a viewer.

What is differentiated in this lesson?

Depending on the choices he or she makes, each student will go through a different process to learn about an artist and gather information for their portraits. Some students will be researching or gathering images, while others will be conducting interviews that lead all students toward the successful creation of a portrait.

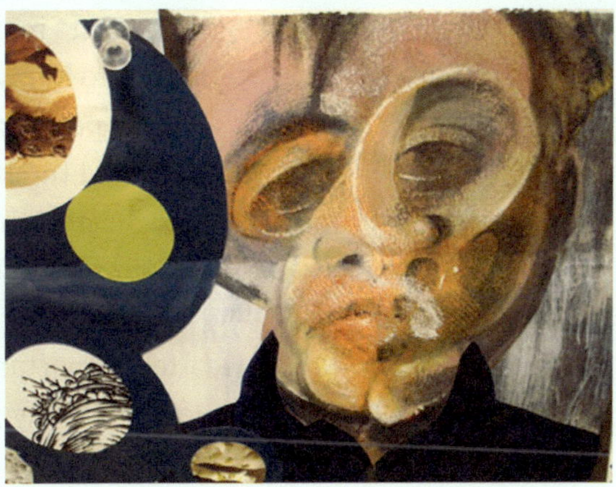

7.16 *Portrait Example.* Photo by Heather L. R. Fountain.

After exploring the three choices, students carefully decided which choice would be most meaningful to them. They were asked to thoughtfully consider and complete the choice sheet about the topic they chose by brainstorming ideas, textures, and any other details that were relevant to their choices. They were directed to "remember that this project is personal and speaks volumes about who you are as an artist and person. Take it seriously!"

Throughout the next five days, McKerns saw and heard amazing things happening as students worked on their projects. She noted that students could not wait to get into the room and were disappointed to have to clean up at the end of class.

She wrote in her journal, "The students are so excited! I have never had a project where I reached everyone in the room. The students instantly decided which choices were right for them. I got to know my students more than I ever had in only one class period as I met with each to discuss [his or her] choice. The second the kids walked into the room I had them get in a circle to discuss their choices. Every student in the room expressed their ideas and the students were engaged in what their peers were saying. It was truly an incredible moment. Each student felt important and wanted to be heard. I was so happy to hear not only my girls but my boys talking about their memories and sacred objects." As the lesson continued and students worked, she wrote in her journal, "Silence, silence, silence, you can hear a pin drop. The students are so engaged with their projects. The room is so calm and filled with hardworking students."

This lesson helped students to make personal connections to the clay pod project. They walked away not only with techniques, but with a way to process personal things in their lives as well. Some students created a way to remember loved ones who had passed away or to honor important people in their lives. Others found a way to vent secrets or create a home for objects that were important to them. This lesson—one that had resulted in many abandoned pods in the artroom the year before—became an amazing lesson that reached beyond the classroom to touch not only the lives of the students involved, but also extended friends and family.

McKerns shared that not one pod was left behind at the end of this project, compared to twenty-nine the year before. This was a clear testament to how much this project was valued by the students; their final reflection comments clearly summarized their thoughts:

- I loved coming to school. I couldn't wait for second block.
- This is the only ceramic project I did not give to my mom to put on the shelf. I kept it for myself.
- I couldn't wait for you to show my mom the pod during conferences.
- I never knew people in the class until we talked about the people in their lives who had died.
- My dad cried when I gave him my pod.
- I felt closure about losing my grandmother.

What was differentiated in this lesson?

The process of this lesson was differentiated to ensure that all types of learners could engage in the various aspects of the lesson by experiencing the stations that were designed around the concept of multiple intelligences. The product of this lesson was also differentiated, allowing all students to create very different final products inspired by unique ideas and choices.

THINK POINT

What, How, and Why

Try to think of one lesson that you could modify into a differentiated lesson.

- **What** will you differentiate—the content, the process, or the product?
- **How** will you differentiate—through choice, the use of pre-assessment data, with various modes of engaging students with the learning content, or through the intentional use of learning styles or multiple intelligences preferences?
- **Why** will you differentiate this lesson—to increase student investment, to help students connect in personal ways to the content, to offer students more ownership over their learning, or to help all students be engaged through different modes of learning?

How was the lesson differentiated?

This lesson was differentiated by:

- The pre-assessment of students' multiple intelligences, which was used to form peer groups with varied strengths.
- The creation of six stations based on different MI preference areas that helped students consider lesson-related topics.
- The option of three product choices from which students could choose.

Why was it differentiated?

This lesson was differentiated to:

- Help build personal connections and investment in the assignment and the skills being taught.
- Make the assignment meaningful to all students.
- Help all students be experts by using their MI preferences to assist their team in completing a station that corresponded to their area of greatest strength.
- Help students consider how, with their own unique skills, each person in the class is important to the whole.

MAJOR POINTS

The Hook

Assessing students' interests can help you build learning experiences that connect with students in personal ways. When students are hooked into or excited about what they are learning, they are more likely to be invested in the experience.

Conclusion

What does a differentiated lesson look like? As you can tell from the three examples provided in this chapter, differentiated lessons can be as varied as the individuals in your classroom. There is no one right way to create a differentiated lesson, but there are elements that all differentiated lessons have in common:

1. They include a consideration of who students are and what they need to succeed.
2. They offer different ways of interacting with learning through choice or varied modes of instruction.
3. They include levels of appropriate challenge to help students reach higher levels of achievement.
4. They show respect for students' differences.
5. They try to connect with students in personal ways to help them relate to, or find investment in, learning.
6. They require teachers to plan ahead and step back once in a while to allow students to be leaders and explorers discovering knowledge together.

Notes

1 J. M. Peterson and M. M. Hittie, *Inclusive Teaching: Creating Effective Classrooms for All Learners* (Princeton, NJ: Pearson, 2003): p. xix

2 Kay Toliver, "Fractions: Any Way You Slice It," *The Eddie Files* (Los Angeles: FASE Productions, 1996).

3 Many of the facts for the Let Freedom Ring cards were retrieved from http://www.iabolish.org (accessed November 12, 2011, and May 18, 2012).

REFLECTION & PRACTICE

Planning for Success

1 **Inclusive Teaching** Consider the location where you teach. Does the room have supplies stored in organized and accessible places so that all students can reach them? Are there places in the room where students can sit alone if they need space away from others? Are there places of visual high interest and places of visual calm? Consider the classroom space and figure out if any areas of the room need to be redesigned to help students have access to educational spaces that fit with their learning needs.

2 **Student Engagement** Keep a log or record for one week that notes any students who do not seem to be engaged in your class. It could be a simple color-coded chart with class lists that have a red dot next to each name of a student who seemed bored, a blue dot for those who demanded your attention due to behavior issues, and so forth. Consider what students made you feel frustrated and why? At the end of the week, look at your log to see if any pattern arises. Consider ways to use choice, learning styles, and interests to engage more students.

3 **Differentiation** Try to think of one lesson that you could modify into a differentiated lesson.

a **What will you differentiate:** the *Process*, the *Product* or the *Content?*

b **How will you differentiate:** through choice, with the use of pre-assessment data, by offering various modes of engaging with the learning content, or through the intentional use of learning styles or multiple intelligences preferences?

c **Why will you differentiate this lesson:** to increase student investment, to help students connect in personal ways to the content, to offer students more ownership over their learning, or to help all students be engaged through different modes of learning?

Chapter 8

Tips for Success

"So it is with teaching . . . to neither mourn what we have not done nor to rest on our victories, but to look at all the reasons we have to show up again tomorrow at the classroom door, ready to join our students—all of our students—in learning."

Carol Ann Tomlinson

Making Implementation Work

Have you ever tried something new, only to second-guess yourself the whole time, wondering if you are doing it "right"? This was exactly how I felt when I attended my first yoga class. I was discreetly looking around at everyone else to see if I was on track or making a fool of myself. Of course I looked silly; I was doing the cat and cow poses, trying to stretch while worrying about what my backside looked like to the people behind me. All of a sudden I realized that it didn't really matter if I looked silly because I was new and I was there, in the class, trying my best. No one expected me to be perfect. It is the same when we begin anything new.

Let One Step Lead to Another

"Success is not final, failure is not fatal; it is the courage to continue that counts." Winston Churchill

When you start implementing DI, you may feel the same way I did in yoga, unsure if you are doing it "right." The best piece of advice to help you along is to overcome the idea that you have to be excellent or perfect at it right away. This is the same goal we help our students realize in the art classroom when they get frustrated and quit because something is too hard or they cannot make something look as good as their neighbor's work. Just like making a piece of artwork, it takes time and practice to learn a new skill and make it seem effortless.

Start in a place that makes sense to you. Take one step at a time. You could start by pre-assessing students' readiness for an upcoming topic and using that information to redesign a lesson you have taught before. Maybe you have a lesson that you can differentiate using choices that relate to different learning styles or interests. It doesn't matter where you start,

PERSONAL CONNECTIONS

Sustaining Results

As you read, consider the following questions:

1 Who can you turn to for support and reflection as you implement differentiated instruction?

2 If you had to list your current mission or reasons for teaching art, what would they be?

3 How can you share what you have learned about Differentiated Instruction with others including parents, students, colleagues, and administrators?

just that you do. Every painting, even a Picasso, started with one stroke—and look at what that one stroke became!

Once you get started differentiating your first lesson, challenge yourself to differentiate another, maybe even one in each grade level or topic that you teach. You will quickly find that it becomes easier to differentiate your lessons, and eventually it will just become a part of how you think and operate in your classroom setting.

Find Accountability

It is always easier to try something new when you have a partner to support and encourage you. That person could be a colleague in your school or even in another school. You need at least one other person who is willing to listen honestly to your ideas, successes, and near misses, and give you constructive yet supportive feedback.

If you have ever tried to start a new exercise routine, you know exactly what I mean. You start off with the best intentions, but an overly busy day or an unexpected event and your new exercise routine is set aside "just for a while," which usually turns into much longer. The same thing can happen to your efforts to use DI. You have the best of intentions and start to see the benefits it provides, but then you get busy or overloaded. Maybe you are teaching more students than the year before, or you lost your classroom, or you are trying to include more literacy integration into your lessons. Whatever the case may be, just as with exercise, it can be easy to lay your efforts aside "just for a while" if you don't have a partner to encourage you and remind you of how much you have grown.

When I first began using DI, I was fortunate enough to have a group of teachers in my school who also wanted to learn

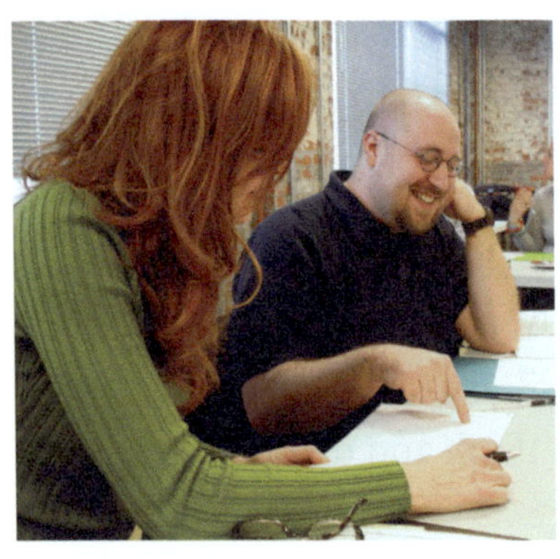

8.1 The support of another teacher can help you gain new perspective and provide needed encouragement.
Photo by Heather L. R. Fountain.

how to use DI in their classrooms. Together, we became a professional learning community. We stayed after school one day a week for ten weeks to learn about DI and create curriculum for our classes, while earning professional development credit. Although I was the only art teacher in this group, my colleagues kept me on task because we all had agreed to share one thing that we had created each week. They also provided the encouragement and feedback I needed to try new things and keep moving forward, even when an idea did not go as planned. This is an ideal supportive situation, but I have also taught in a school where I was the only one who knew about DI. In that case, my dad, a fifth grade science teacher, listened and provided the feedback and encouragement that I needed to keep growing.

You may find yourself in a school that values DI and wants all teachers to use it, or you may be in a school where no one knows about DI. No matter what your situation, it is important for you to find at least one other like-minded individual who will be excited about what you are doing and will listen and provide feedback with caring honesty. Don't discount people simply because they don't teach your subject, as they can provide a perspective that can be extremely valuable.

Be Respectful to Others Who May or May Not Want to Differentiate Instruction

It is important to remember that even adults learn differently. It is easy to forget that teachers, like our students, have different learning styles and respond differently to new things. If you look at your colleagues, you will find that there are those who are eager to jump in and try new things right away. Some will need the support of a friend or colleague. Others will see the results of change and then be convinced it is worth their time. There are always people who need to watch and wait for a long time in order to make up their minds. There are even those, hopefully a minority, who want no part of anything new.

Your colleagues may be excited about trying DI along with you, but many will need to see DI in action before jumping in. It is important to respect those around you and allow people the space and time they need to decide if DI is something they want to know more about. It is common for teachers who are new to DI to see amazing things happen in their own classrooms and want others around them to share in their success. It is fine to be excited about what is happening in your room, but be sure to share it in ways that do not threaten others or make them feel like they are not good teachers because they are not using DI.

THEORIES & TERMS

Universal Design vs. Differentiated Instruction

Universal Design, a term coined by architect Ronald Mace, refers to the design of products and environments that people of all ages and abilities can use to the greatest extent possible.[1] Although originally developed for use in architecture and eventually commercial design, Universal Design has been widely applied to other fields including education.

Universal Design as applied in Education (UDE) is the creation of an educational experience in which all aspects are accessible to all individuals involved, with consideration given to issues related to gender, race, ethnicity, age, physical ability, and learning style.[2]

How does Universal Design in Education compare to Differentiated Instruction? The core values of UDE and DI are the same—valuing individuals and creating ways for all people, no matter who they are, to access educational experiences successfully. While UDE focuses on the areas of teaching, curriculum, assessment, space, resources, and communication, DI goes beyond those aspects to consider students in more specific ways as contributing partners in their learning. Teachers who use DI find that they get to know their students very personally and can use that information to motivate and engage them, while holding them to high, yet attainable, standards.

If you make it known that you are universally designing curriculum to meet the needs of all students through the use of DI, then your colleagues will know who to ask if they want to learn more. Your colleagues will also hear about what is happening in your classroom from others—parents, visitors, other teachers, and even your students—and may ask you to share more information with them. You may even have someone pop into your room to see what is going on. Invite them to join in and become part of a group, even if it is for just a moment.

Make an Action Plan

John F. Kennedy once said, "Efforts and courage are not enough without purpose and direction."[3] Having a purpose or direction as a guide is certainly important in helping us accomplish our goals. When we go on a trip, we get directions, use a map or GPS, or talk to others who have been there before us. Even if we get lost, we can refer to a map and find our way back. If you don't know where you are going, you are bound to wander aimlessly or get lost along the way. Having a plan for implementing DI will help you stay focused on your goals and make it more likely that you will attain them.

State Your Mission

Most organizations or businesses have a mission statement that expresses the core beliefs and goals of the group. Mission statements help to ensure that there is clarity in the direction that the group will take. They can be as simple as a sentence, a paragraph, or even a bulleted list of items. For example, the core of Disney's mission statement is "to make people happy."[4] Mission statements can also inspire and help provide focus when needed. In order to succeed over the long term, you must

THINK POINT

Writing a Mission Statement

If you need help designing a DI mission statement, let the following three areas guide you:

Vision What is the big-picture idea of what you want to achieve for both you and your students? What is most important to you as a teacher?

Mission Where do you want to go? What is your general plan for how you will achieve your vision?

Core Values What behaviors or beliefs will guide you in this process? What reasons do you have for improving your curriculum? Why is using DI important to you and your students? Why is it worth your time?

know what you value and how you intend to achieve it. What are your core beliefs and goals as an educator?

Take the time to create your own DI mission statement and place it in a location where you can review it on a regular basis. If you get discouraged or begin to question why you are taking the time to differentiate, you can stop, read your statement, and regain clarity about your mission.

Set Attainable Goals

In graduate school, I heard educational leader Ted Sizer say that "true change takes time." This is a wonderful reminder that we need to allow ourselves time to learn and grow. You can't expect to be able to implement everything you have learned about DI at once; you will need to set small, attainable goals.

This point became all the more evident to me when I first read *The Genesis of a Painting: Picasso's Guernica*.[5] Even Picasso, a man widely acknowledged as a master artist and innovator, created numerous sketches of the elements of *Guernica* before completing the mural. I remember looking through the book and counting twelve sketches of just the horse. Picasso said that paintings themselves, in addition to sketches, were his research and experimentation. Think of each small step you take to implement Differentiated Instruction as research or experimentation to assist you on your journey.

Decide on Short- and Long-Term Goals

Think about the goals you would like to accomplish and sort them into two categories, short-term goals and long-term goals. If you are not sure where to start, set one attainable goal for your first month. My first goal was to create a set of choice cards for an existing lesson. After implementing my new variation on an old lesson, I realized that I needed to have a top card in the set with clear steps and directions for students to follow. I was able to make this adjustment fairly easily before the next group of students came in to start that lesson.

After you set an initial goal, try to think of what you would like to achieve with your implementation of DI in three months, six months, and by the end of a school year. Once you have completed a school year, you will be able to sort through your first differentiated lessons and refine them to make them better for the next school year or create new ones to add to your repertoire.

If you don't already do this, set goals for yourself at the start of each school year. Be sure to set check-in dates where you review your goals and monitor your progress. Although you will always find ways to improve your teaching, remember to celebrate the small accomplishments along the way. If you do not meet a goal on your list during the school year, reevaluate it to see if you can realistically attain it. If it is an important goal, add it to next year's list; if not, move on.

Advocacy: Helping Others See the Value of Differentiated Instruction

By definition, advocacy is the active support for an idea or cause. In the arts, we are very familiar with this concept. In fact, people and groups have been advocating for the arts in public schools since the 1800s. In many cases, advocacy is the difference between cutting school art programs or saving them. Advocacy, whether strident or unassuming, can influence public opinion, help garner support, and generate resources for a cause. Or, it can simply inform people about a proposal that has great value. As with the arts, you can advocate for DI with simple steps that can also build advocacy for your art program. These steps will help people understand what DI is and how valuable it can be in helping students learn through the arts. The following are a few ideas on how to initiate advocacy:

Include parent helpers in your room. As parents see productive, excited students working in your room, the word will spread about how amazing the art teacher and art classes are in your school. This can only help parents see the value of art for their children. I have often had parent volunteers in my room and I have even had a room parent who would get the word out to other parents when I needed special things or help for events. At first, I valued the few extra hands that parents' help could provide, but later I realized that these parents were more than helpers, they were reporters and advocates. The wisest teachers know that they teach parents as well as children.

One day, a parent came into my room and told me that I was the topic of a conversation at a soccer game the night before. Apparently, one mother made a negative comment about how she was "unsure about that art teacher lady" her daughter had. Overhearing this, a few moms, two of whom were volunteers in my room, assured her that I was "awesome" and doing amazing things in the artroom. Parent advocacy can stretch beyond the school's walls onto the soccer field or even into a school board meeting. Never underestimate the advocacy that parents can provide.

Invite your principal, vice-principal, supervisor, or the superintendent to observe your room and provide you with feedback. Let them know you have been trying to implement DI as a way to help all students connect with learning in meaningful ways. If they have not heard of DI, leave an information sheet on your desk that they can read when they observe your class so they will know what you are doing and why. Chances are that if they don't know about DI, it will pique their interest enough for them to read up on it.

A young teacher I coached on the use of DI used this strategy with her principal and found herself with a lifelong supporter. After his visit, the principal knew that she was doing amazing things and regularly popped into her classroom to see what was going on, even when he became the superintendent of the district. Her classroom also served as a model classroom that other teachers visited to learn more about DI. This type of advocacy made it possible for her to accomplish many special lessons and events because her principal believed in what she was doing. Extra resources became available to help her accomplish many of her ideas.

Share a success with other teachers. Without bragging or trying to sell DI, share with your colleagues a successful differentiated lesson that went well. At lunch one day, a colleague of mine came in and stated, "I had the most amazing experience this morning. My students were working on different choice options. I looked around and they were all busy, focused, excited, and respectful of each other. I got to actually just walk around my room and see what everyone was doing and talk to them about their plans."

If you share a success, often people want to know more about it and how it came about. Who knows—colleagues might even want to come in and observe what is going on in your classroom.

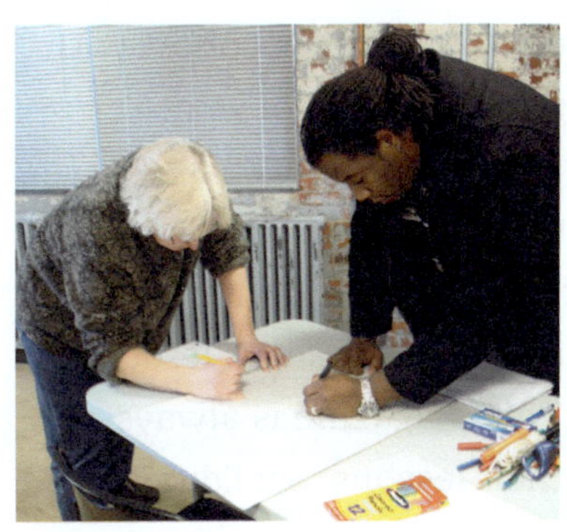

8.2 Professional learning communities are a great way for teachers to learn and grow together, while helping each other accomplish important teaching goals. Photo by Heather L. R. Fountain.

Create a professional learning community or book club. Many schools are encouraging teachers to develop professional learning communities. These can take a variety of forms, but often a professional community revolves around a book or reading topic. Create your own group and invite others to learn about DI with you. As a professional community, you will be able to support each other and share ideas to help each other grow.

Place an article in the school newsletter, blog, or webpage about a lesson or event that involved your students. This is an easy way to let parents know how DI is shaping art education. It is best to keep what you share simple and positive, concentrating on how their children's learning is your focus. Visuals are always helpful. Be sure to share what you have written with your principal or supervisor and ask for permission before posting it.

Display students' differentiated products in the community. Libraries, school district offices, municipal buildings, or other community locations often seek out artwork to display. When preparing a display, be sure to include what the lesson was about, the choices students had, and a small paragraph about DI that explains your lesson design. This is just another way to help people see and understand what DI has to offer. It also gets your name out in the community.

Host an in-service event for the other art teachers in your district on inclusive teaching through DI. If you have a room, host the event in your classroom so everyone can see what is happening there. You could share the lessons and results of implementing DI in your classroom. This will help those who need to see DI in practice understand not only what your goals were, but exactly how you accomplished them and with what results. This could

MAJOR POINTS

Long-Term Success

School reformer and educator Ted Sizer said that true change takes time. To help yourself create true, sustainable changes in your teaching or even in your school, allow yourself to take one step at a time building a strong foundation of ideas and strategies before moving onto the next step. Try on a strategy, test it out, assess the outcomes, and adjust it as needed before moving on to other ideas. As you continually reflect on the changes you implement, keep in mind that it helps to have the support of others around you with whom you can discuss ideas, talk through challenges, or who can help you gain new perspectives on your ideas.

also provide you with an opportunity to meet a DI cohort with whom you can shares ideas throughout the school year.

Publish a differentiated lesson or strategy in an art education magazine or on Art Ed. 2.0. SchoolArts magazine is an art education publication that serves as a place to share lessons and ideas with other art teachers. This magazine is always looking for teachers to contribute their lessons. *Art Education 2.0* is an international online art education community where educators can share ideas and connect with each other. If you search *groups* on the site, you will find DI professionals.

Give a DI presentation at a local or national conference. I have designed some of my best ideas for lessons from strategies I learned from others. When we see or hear about successes in someone else's classroom, it can ignite in us a passion for teaching and learning, a passion we can share with our students. Again, this is another way to help others see how DI functions in your room. Be sure to have visuals and, if possible, include a specific strategy you used with your students as well as their responses to DI.

By presenting at a national conference, a graduate student of mine was able to share her experience with other teachers. She provided a video documentation of her experience and that of another colleague at a different school using DI in the art classroom, and she included the reactions of her students. She noted that presenting at the conference was extremely valuable because it enabled her to connect with other teachers from around the country, some of whom she corresponded with through e-mail after she went home.

Conclusion

There are many excellent DI curriculum ideas and programs out there that are working. They all have one thing in common—valuing students for the people they are, and helping them connect in meaningful ways to what they are learning. DI is not a specific program or a set of lesson plans that you can follow. It does not tell you what to do or when to do it; it is a guide that takes the best practices in education and combines them into a core set of values, competencies, suggestions, and strategies that will help you create powerful learning experiences for your students.

DI made me feel like a better teacher. It helped me to accomplish my goals of reaching and teaching all of my students about art. It helped me to find ways to turn art from something to fear into an enjoyable, engaging subject for everyone, not just those who are "talented." It helped me take my lessons to deeper levels and build upon my students' prior knowledge. It gave me a classroom where students wanted to be, even if they didn't want to be in school. It created a space where all voices were truly valued; and people's differences were seen as unique characteristics, not as reasons to denigrate or exclude anyone. It gave me time with my students because I had almost no behavioral issues to deal with. It gave me what I had always wanted, a classroom of students who were eager to learn about and make art.

When you show your students that they—their ideas, their learning needs, their backgrounds, their voices, and their interests—are important to you, they will know that you care about them. At our core, we all just want to be noticed, loved, and cared for; that is the powerful message that DI uses to transform classrooms and schools into amazing communities of learners.

If you have made it to the end of this book and you are still wondering, "How can I do this when I have so much prescribed curriculum to teach?" I will tell you what I have seen again and again: The beauty of DI is that you can use it to teach any topic or subject, to any age. It won't tell you what to teach or when, like a curriculum guide, but it will help you figure out how to teach any topic in powerful and effective ways.

If you or your colleagues are worried about teaching to a test, rest assured that both low- and high-performing schools that committed to using DI had marked increases in their standardized test scores.[6] When teachers and students in my school began to worry about the new state standardized tests because we were using DI and not teaching in more conventional ways, our principal read us a book to help us find comfort and security. She knew that we were doing what was best for our students by using DI, even if our teaching methods looked different from those in other schools. I hope you, too, will find comfort in some of the words that she shared with us from the Dr. Seuss book *Hooray for Diffendoofer Day!*[7]

> Our school is at the corner of Dinkerzoober and Dinkerzott. It looks like any other school, but we suspect it's not. I think we are learning many things not taught in other schools. Our teachers are remarkable; they make up their own rules....We were eating our concoctions, telling jokes and making noise, when Mr. Lowe appeared and howled, "Attention girls and boys!" All schools for miles and miles around must take a special test to see who's learning such and such—to see

> which school's the best....Miss Bonkers rose. "Don't fret!" she said. "You've learned the things you need to pass that test and many more—I'm certain you'll succeed. We've taught you that the earth is round, that red and white make pink. And something else that matters more—We've taught you how to *think*."

Be courageous in your teaching, knowing that you are helping your students not only to learn about art, but also how to think, to become lifelong learners and people who respect those around them for who they are—even if they are different.

REFLECTION & PRACTICE

Sustaining Results

1 **Accountability** Support is key in helping teachers reflect and continue to improve their teaching practice; who can you count on to provide support and honest feedback about your teaching? Make a list of people who could provide you with support.

Keep in mind that different people can provide different levels of support. Some might be there to lend an ear, others might be walking the path with you in their own classroom practice. They could be in your school or field of study or not; either way consider all possible supporters and add them to your list. Make a plan to talk to and find at least two people who can support your growth as a teacher.

2 **Mission and Action Plan** In order to succeed long term you must know what you value. What are your core beliefs and goals as an educator? Take time to create your own Differentiated Instruction mission statement and place it in a location where you can see it on a regular basis. Attach to it an action plan of what you hope to accomplish through DI in three months, six months, and one year. Be sure to revisit it and revise it yearly.

3 **Advocacy** How will you share the amazing things that are happening in your classroom through the use of DI? How will you help students, parents, colleagues, and administrators understand what DI is, and what it is adding to the educational experiences in your school? Consider the advocacy tips in this chapter and implement at least two this school year.

Notes

1 M. F. Story, J. L. Mueller, and R. L. Mace, *The Universal Design File: Designing for People of All Ages and Abilities* (Raleigh, NC: North Carolina State University, 1998).

2 S. Burgstahler, *Universal Design in Education: Principles and Applications* (Seattle, WA: University of Washington, 2009). http://design.ncsu.edu/cud/pubs_p/pudfiletoc.htm (accessed November 25, 2011).

3 From a campaign speech in Raleigh, NC, Sept. 17, 1960.

4 Http://www.nacada.ksu.edu/clearinghouse/Advisingissues/Mission-Statements.htm (accessed May 18, 2012).

5 R. Arnheim, *The Genesis of a Painting: Picasso's Guernica* (Berkeley, CA: University of California Press, 1962).

6 C. A. Tomlinson, K. Brimijoin, and L. Narvaez, *The Differentiated School: Making Revolutionary Changes in Teaching and Learning* (Alexandria, VA: Association for Supervision and Curriculum Development, 2008).

7 Dr. Seuss, J. Prelutsky, and L. Smith, *Hooray for Diffendoofer Day!* (New York: Random House Children's Books, 2008).

Appendix

Download reproducible resources and worksheets at Davisart.com/Differentiated

The following pages can be photocopied at 125% to fit on standard letter paper (8.5 x 11 inches).

Museum Guide Sheet

A.5.1

One thing I want you to know about me is that...

My favorite item or items in the exhibition are: (Please explain)...

Something else I want you to know while viewing my museum exhibition is...

The title of my personal art museum exhibition is:

____

The artist and curator of this exhibition is:

____

What Makes Me ME

A.5.2

Name: ______________________ **Class:** ______________________

Answer honestly and appropriately (in accordance with our existing rules of conduct). Our classes will include ideas and learning that relate to the views you share here.

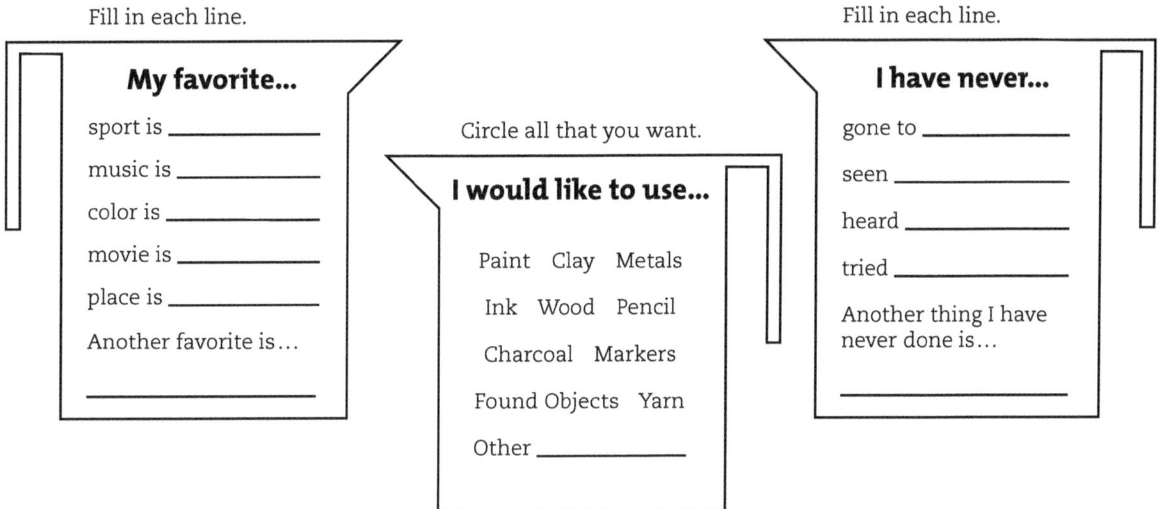

Recipe for a successful class...

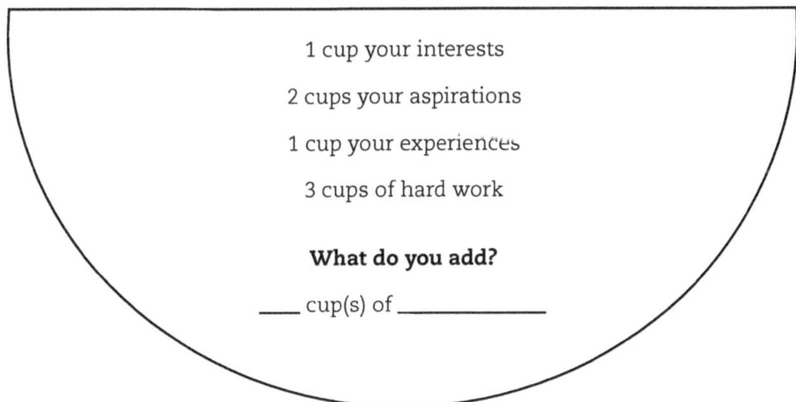

Mix well, bring to a boil, then enjoy our class!

What's My Learning Style?

A.5.3a

Look through the statements below and put an X in the box by the ones that best describe you. If you see something that you do, but only once in a while, skip it and choose the answers that relate to things you do most often. When you are done, look at the *What's My Learning Style?* sheet (A.5.7b) and match your answers to the ones below to discover your learning-style preference.

☐ I need to hear it to remember it.

☐ I often need to talk through what I am thinking in order to understand it.

☐ I remember things best when I repeat them to myself.

☐ I prefer to listen to books.

☐ It helps me to talk things through to solve problems or figure things out.

☐ I am good at remembering what people say.

☐ It helps me to understand things when I see a picture or example.

☐ I often draw things out to explain them to other people.

☐ I am drawn to colors or other visually appealing things.

☐ Sometimes I appear to be daydreaming, but really I am trying to visualize something in my head.

☐ I remember things best when I can see the person who is speaking.

☐ I remember where things are located on a page.

☐ I need to write out information to help me understand it.

☐ It helps me remember things when I have something in writing to refer back to.

☐ I am often quiet or introverted.

☐ I like to take notes and collect written material.

☐ I enjoy using the Internet to discover or read things.

☐ It helps me when teachers post directions, objectives, or other project steps on the board.

☐ I learn best when I can physically do something, not just listen.

☐ I have difficulty staying still for more than a few minutes.

☐ I often ignore directions and start working right away independently.

☐ I prefer to hear or read stories that are full of action.

☐ If I can make, create, or do something, it helps me process and remember what I am learning.

☐ I like to play sports, dance, or do other things where I can move around.

What's My Learning Style? – Teacher

A.5.3b

Look through the statements below and put an X by the ones that match your answers marked on the front of this sheet. The category with the most marked answers will tell you your preferred learning style.

Visual

- ☐ It helps me to understand things when I see a picture or example.
- ☐ I often draw things out to explain them to other people.
- ☐ I am drawn to colors or other visually appealing things.
- ☐ Sometimes I appear to be daydreaming, but really I am trying to visualize something in my head.
- ☐ I remember things best when I can see the person who is speaking.
- ☐ I remember where things are located on a page.

Kinesthetic

- ☐ I learn best when I can physically do something, not just listen.
- ☐ I have difficulty staying still for more than a few minutes.
- ☐ I often ignore directions and start working right away independently.
- ☐ I prefer to hear or read stories that are full of action.
- ☐ If I can make, create, or do something, it helps me process and remember what I am learning.
- ☐ I like to play sports, dance, or do other things where I can move around.

Written

- ☐ I need to write out information to help me understand it.
- ☐ It helps me remember things when I have something in writing to refer back to.
- ☐ I am often quiet or introverted.
- ☐ I like to take notes and collect written material.
- ☐ I enjoy using the Internet to discover or read things.
- ☐ It helps me when teachers post directions, objectives, or other project steps on the board.

Auditory

- ☐ I need to hear it to remember it.
- ☐ I often need to talk through what I am thinking in order to understand it.
- ☐ I remember things best when I repeat them to myself.
- ☐ I prefer to listen to books.
- ☐ It helps me to talk things through to solve problems or figure things out.
- ☐ I am good at remembering what people say.

My name is: ____________________

My preferred learning style is: ____________________

Oral Learning Style Inventory

A.5.4

Name: **Class:**

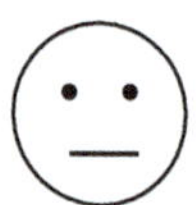

1.

2.

3.

4.

5.

6.

7.

8.

9.

10.

11.

12.

13.

14.

15.

16.

17.

Ask students the following questions, and ask them to draw their response (smiley, ho-hum, or sad face) next to the corresponding number.

How do you feel about…

1. Drawing or coloring?
2. Looking at artwork?
3. Talking with other people?
4. Being by yourself?
5. Being with other people?
6. Reading?
7. Writing?
8. Listening to stories?
9. Dancing or moving around?
10. Using numbers?
11. Listening to music?
12. Making music?
13. Playing games or sports?
14. Computers?
15. Being a leader?
16. Helping others?
17. Thinking about things?

To use this as a handout for students, cover these instructions before copying.

Planning for Differentiation by Learning Style Using Four Square

A.5.5a

Name: ______________________ **Class:** ______________________

Being Unique: Identity is shaped by our unique qualities and experiences.

Essential Questions:

What is unique or special about you?
What makes you different from others?
What makes you similar to others?
What people have an effect on who you are?

Key Concepts:

Identity is shaped by things and people around us.
We shape our identity.
Our interests shape our identity.
We have our own unique identity but some parts of it might overlap with others.

Objectives:

Know

- Students will explore the concept of how identity is shaped both internally and externally (by themselves and by others) by writing on a Frayer Diagram or concept map.

Understand

- Students will discuss, with one or more people, the most important person, group of people, or thing that has affected their identity and how.

Do

- Students will create a design that represents who they are through the use of images that have been chosen for specific purposes.
- With care, students will use their design to create a unique screen print that represents their identity.
- Students will demonstrate tool safety by using tools correctly and responsibly through the duration of their projects.
- Students will share their identity screen print with peers through a pair-share or group-share activity in which they explain one or more of the choices they have made and why it represents an important part of their identity.

Planning for Differentiation Using Four Square—Example

A.5.5b

Name: ______________________ **Class:** ______________________

Visual

Create a visually engaging mixed media collage piece that represents who you are as an artist to display with your screen print.

Kinesthetic

Use the class camera or your own equipment to video tape your artist statement. Be sure to make it engaging for your viewer.

Written

To accompany your screen print, create an artist statement. You can use poetry, creative writing, or informative writing. Be sure it is at least one page.

Auditory

Develop an artist statement that can be listened to by the viewer. You may incorporate, your voice, the voices of others, music, and sounds as needed to convey your message.

Planning for Differentiation by Learning Style (Four Square)

A.5.5c

Name: ______________________ **Class:** ______________________

Visual

Kinesthetic

Written

Auditory

WOW! You *Are* Smart!

A.5.6

Name: ______________________ **Class:** ______________________

1. Fold the paper vertically on the dark line so that the Multiple Intelligences (MI) answers are hidden.
2. Read each statement below and decide if it sounds most like you.
3. If it sounds most like you, then place an X next to that statement.
4. When you have finished all the statements, unfold your paper and count up how many answers about you fit in each category. You are probably smart in all these ways, but in some areas more than others.

Which statements are true for you?

		MI
I love listening to music.		M/R
I like to work with other people.		IEP
Seeing things in writing or writing things down helps me think.		V/L
My best way to learn is through hands-on activities.		B/K
I can read maps easily.		V/S
Having quiet time to think through ideas is really important to me.		IAP
I love math.		L/M
I enjoy singing or writing songs.		M/R
I like to collect things from nature like shells or rocks.		N/E
I like drama or acting things out with gestures.		B/K
It helps me to draw things out when I an explaining them to others.		V/S
I enjoy problem solving and brain teasers.		L/M
I like spending time by myself.		IAP
I would love playing musical instruments or think I would.		M/R
I am good at writing stories or plays.		V/L
I keep a diary or journal.		IAP
I am good at dancing or other sports.		B/K
My friends often come to me to talk when they have problems or need help.		IEP
I like being outside in nature.		N/E
I am often humming, tapping a beat, or singing to myself.		M/R
I love caring for pets and other animals.		N/E
It helps to me see pictures or examples when I am learning.		V/S
I care about the environment so much that I must do something to protect it.		N/E
I like to be able to move around, and when I do, I rarely bump into others.		B/K
I enjoy crossword puzzles or word games.		V/L
I am good at figuring out patterns.		L/M
I am good at understanding other points of view even if they're different from my own.		IEP
I feel very sad when others are hurting, and I want to help them feel better.		IEP
I understand math easily, even when others around me have a hard time.		L/M
I enjoy reading.		V/L
I like writing about my thoughts and feelings.		IAP
Graphic organizers or mind maps help me think through ideas.		V/S

N/E ____ L/M ____ V/L ____ V/S ____ IAP ____ IEP ____ B/K ____ M/R ____

Planning for Differentiation by Multiple Intelligences Preference

A.5.7a

Verbal/Linguistic

Write a poem about patterns. Create three or more pictures to go with it. Be ready to share your pictures and your poem with someone else.

Bodily/Kinesthetic

Gather four things from around the room or from the pattern grab bag. Draw three patterns that you can make with these items, and then return them to where they came from.

Logical/Mathematical

Pretend you are the teacher today. Place an "X" over all incorrect answers on the pattern sheet. Count up how many are wrong. Correct the mistakes you found, so your student will know how to fix them.

Intrapersonal

Are there patterns in your life? Think of three patterns that are part of your life and draw them.

Big Idea/Lesson

Pattern Exploration

Grade 1

Interpersonal

Write a story about patterns. Use pictures of patterns in your presentation.

Musical/Rhythmical

Write a song about patterns to share with your class. Create at least four pictures to go with your song.

Naturalistic

Draw and color four things from nature that show pattern.

Visual/Spatial

Create a new logo for a crayon company that includes at least three patterns. Use construction paper to create a new crayon box with your design on it.

Goals

To gain a basic understanding of patterns.

To explore patterns of various kinds in art and in our world.

To have students create at least two patterns.

Special thanks to Marcie Kuhns for assistance with this lesson idea.

Planning for Differentiation by Multiple Intelligences Preference

A.5.7b

Verbal/Linguistic	Bodily/Kinesthetic	Logical/Mathematical
Intrapersonal	Big Idea/Lesson	**Interpersonal**
Musical/Rhythmical	**Naturalistic**	**Visual/Spatial**

Goals

Station #1: Monoprint

A.6.1a

A monoprint is a print that happens once (mono).

1. The artist paints or rolls ink quickly onto a smooth, washable surface, such as a tabletop or a piece of glass or Plexiglas (*printing plate*).
2. The artist adds or wipes away paint until satisfied with the texture or image created.
3. The artist then places a piece of paper over the image and carefully rubs its entire surface to ensure the paper has come in contact with the painted printing plate.
4. Finally, the artist peels the paper off the printing plate to reveal the print. The artist can rework the printing plate with additional ink or paint, or wash off and dry the printing plate and start over again.

Tip

Sometimes it is possible to create a *ghost print*. Once the artist smoothes the paper over the printing plate and lifts it off, a second piece of paper is immediately placed on the image, creating a print that is always much lighter than the first—a ghost image.

Vocabulary

monoprint

printing plate

ghost print

Create

1. Cover the table with newspaper.
2. Create one or two monoprints of your own. If you need an idea, create a scene of your favorite place or animal. You can also simply explore lines and shapes to create interesting abstract images.
3. When you are done, please clean up this station and leave it ready for the next group (clean and dry tools, clean paper, clean printing plates, and put down new newspaper).

Station #2: Stamping

A.6.1b

One of the most widely used forms of printmaking is stamping. To create a stamp, a shape or image is carved into wood, linoleum, rubber, or cut out of foam, a potato, an eraser or a sponge (the printing plate). Many found objects can be used as a stamp. The surface of the stamp is covered with marker, ink, or paint and pressed onto a surface, creating a pattern or design. The beauty of stamping is that you can quickly create the same image multiple times with ease. You can also clean off your stamp and use it again. Unlike a monoprint (a print that happens only once) you can create multiples.

1. As a group read about *adinkra* on the information sheet at this station.
2. In the *adinkra* cloth nine-block image, choose a design and interpret its meaning by finding the symbols on one of the symbol charts or in the African symbol book.
3. As a group, discuss the following questions:
    a. Why do you think the Ghanaian people created such beautiful cloth to say goodbye to a loved one who had died?
    b. Why do you think the purpose of *adinkra* cloth has changed over time?
    c. What symbolic meaning would you share with others to represent your personality on an *adinkra* cloth?
4. Use stamps to create your own *adinkra* cloth.
    a. Pay attention to the symbols you use, as each will represent you and your beliefs.
    b. Include a border around your block patterns to hold in your beliefs.

Tip

Often you can use the same stamp multiple times before you need to re-ink it. Just keep in mind that each print will be lighter, as less ink will be present on the stamp. Many artists use this to create contrast and interest in their designs.

Vocabulary

Ghana	Ghanaian
printing plate	stamping
adinkra	monoprint
contrast	interest

Extra Challenge: Create a Stamp

1. Draw a small shape in pencil on a piece of foam.
2. Use scissors to cut out your shape.
3. Peel off the white paper from the back of the foam to reveal a sticky surface.
4. Stick your shape to the outside of one of the bottle caps.

YEAH!

You have created your own stamp and are ready to apply marker to it and press it onto the paper. If you want to change colors you MUST completely wash and dry your stamp before using a different colored marker on the surface. Using your stamp, and the ones provided, you can create a beautiful patterned image.

Station #3: Collograph

A.6.1c

Collograph printing is a method of printmaking that uses cardboard and other flat scraps, with or without texture, to create a printing plate. Miró was a surrealist artist who used collograph prints to create imaginary worlds and creatures.

1. In the book *Imagine That!: Activities and Adventures in Surrealism* by Joyce Raimondo, turn to pages 26 and 27.
2. As a group read about Joan Miró.
3. As a team follow the directions to play the Looking Game.
4. After you have made a title for Miró's art scene and described your choice, look below for directions on how to create your own collograph plate. Two examples of collograph prints are at the station, so you can see what a collograph print looks like once it is printed.

Vocabulary

collograph

printing plate

print

Joan Miró

surrealist

Create

1. Use oaktag from an old folder to cut out a rectangle printing plate.
2. Write your name on the back of the plate.
3. Cut out shapes using the oak tag scraps or collect textured materials such string, netting, bubble wrap, foil, or cardboard.
4. Make a printing plate. Cut your materials into shapes and arrange them on the printing plate to create a strange creature.
5. Securely glue down all of your materials onto the plate.
6. Let your collograph print plate dry completely
7. Next class we will print with your collograph plates.

Cube Template

A.6.2

To create your cube, write one cubing choice in each box and cut out the entire shape. Fold on the solid lines and glue or tape the small tabs (dotted lines) in place.

Think-Tac-Toe Example

A.6.3

Color, Emotion, and Composition

Complete one choice in each category. Place a light X over each choice you make. Be sure your name and class designation are on the back of each assignment. Keep this sheet in your folder.

Color	Find ten other artworks that have a color scheme similar to the work provided. List the colors they share and create a title that best describes this color scheme.	Create a new 4 x 4" artwork, using colored pencils. Your artwork should have the same color scheme or palette as the artwork provided.	You are a profiler: write and illustrate a complete and useful profile of the artist who made this piece. Make your profile assumptions based on the artist's use of color.
Emotion	Find pictures of people whose emotions make them look like they belong in this artwork. Cut out the images and create a crowd scene. Use watercolors to paint the background to fit with the emotion of the artwork.	Create a nonrepresentational drawing that conveys the opposite emotion of the artwork provided. Use any medium you wish.	Write a poem that explores or conveys the same emotions that you feel this artwork conveys. Illustrate your poem using any medium you wish.
Composition	Create a sculpture that, when viewed from one specific angle, shares the same basic composition as this work.	Redraw this artwork in a way that shows all of its original parts and elements, but creates a new composition. Be sure to write the reasons for your choices on the back in pencil.	Write a two-page letter to a friend describing this artwork's composition and comparing it to another artwork of your choosing.

Developed and used with the permission of Nick Urffer.

Art Criticism RAFT

A.6.4

Directions:

1. Choose one image of an artwork from the folder on your table.

2. In your journal, record the title of the artwork you chose and write at least two complete sentences in each of the following art criticism categories:

   a. Describe: Tell what you see—the visual facts.

   b. Analyze: Explain how the artist used the elements and principles of art in the piece.

   c. Interpret: Describe what you think the artist was trying to say. What is the meaning of the piece?

   d. Judge: Give your opinion of the artwork based on what you have discovered about it.

Be sure to back up all your answers with evidence.

3. Once you have completed step #2, you may choose one *Role* from the chart below to help you practice talking about and critiquing an artwork. Keep in mind that you will be sharing your choice with others in the class who may have made the same choice.

Role	**A**udience	**F**ormat	**T**opic
The artist who created the artwork	Self	A journal entry	Here is what I need to change about this work:
The artist's teacher	Current students	Formal critique of a work of art	What I like about this work and/or what I don't like.
The artist's significant other	Art critic	Interview for a magazine	Exploring the meaning behind the work
A visitor to a museum seeing the artwork for the first time	A small child	An informal conversation	I wonder why...

Setting the Scene

A.6.5a

Name: **Class:**

Fill in the information to describe the setting of the story in the artwork.

Title of artwork ____________________

What time of day is it?	**Where does the story take place?**	**Who are the important characters or stars?**
____________	____________ ____________	____________ ____________

What do you think happens next?
Sketch a picture to describe your answer.

What surprised you or interested you about this setting? If you could visit this setting, would you want to? Why or why not?

Setting Map

A.6.5b

Name: ______________________ **Class:** ______________________

Title of artwork ______________________

Important characters ______________________

What time of day is it?

____

____

Where does the story take place?

____

____

How important is time to the story? How would the story change if it were a different time?

How is the place important to the story?

How do the characters act or behave because of the time and place in which they live?

Setting, Events, and Character Actions

A.6.5c

Name: **Class:**

Title of artwork ___________

Fill in the chart below. Describe the setting using details from what you see in the artwork, summarize an event, and explain how the setting influenced the characters' actions.

SETTING Fill in all the details you can to describe the setting.	**EVENT** Describe a main event that occurred in this setting.	**CHARACTER ACTION** Describe how the setting influenced the characters' actions in this event.
Place		
Time		
Weather/Climate		
Other things you notice		

Could this event have taken place in a different setting? Yes? No? Explain your answer.

Freedom

A.7.1

Name: **Class:**

Write a definition, in your own words, for freedom.

What are the benefits of freedom?

What are the costs of freedom?

Let Freedom Ring Cards

A.7.2

Give each student in the class a card with one of the following facts to consider:

Contrary to popular belief, slavery occurs on all six inhabited continents. Experts estimate that today there are 27 million people enslaved around the world. And yes, that includes the United States. Slavery did not end in the United States with Abraham Lincoln's Emancipation Proclamation in 1863.	The U.S. Central Intelligence Agency estimates 14,500 to 17,000 victims are trafficked (sold as slaves) into the "land of the free" every year.	In many countries, children can only go to school if their families have the money for tuition, supplies, and uniforms. In China alone, nearly 2 million children are missing out on school because their parents cannot afford tuition fees ($36.00 US).
Approximately 4,484 American troops died in Iraq between 2003 and 2011.	Approximately 33,186 American soldiers were wounded in the Iraq War between 2003 and 2011.	Approximately 2.5 million people have lost their freedom because they are in jail or prison in the United States. That is 1 in 100 adults.
Our country is called "the land of the free," yet we have hundreds of thousands of laws at the city, county, state, and federal levels.	If you are from the country of Haiti and you live in the Dominican Republic, you are not allowed to go to school or to be treated in a hospital (except one mission hospital in La Romana).	Around the globe, millions of children are sold into slavery every day.

Note: Many of the facts for the Let Freedom Ring cards were retrieved from http://www.iabolish.org (accessed November 12, 2011, and May 18, 2012).

Freedom Choice Board

A.7.3

Choice 1	Choice 2	Choice 3
Choice 1 Visit the Norman Rockwell Museum website. View and read about Norman Rockwell's paintings titled *Four Freedoms*. Are these the four freedoms you would have chosen? If yes, describe why; if no, write about or sketch what four freedoms you believe *all* people should have.	**Choice 2** Describe a personal freedom. Illustrate, in words and through the creation of an artwork, one freedom that you wish you had that you currently do not have, or a freedom that you wish all people had in our world. What are some ways that people could achieve this freedom?	**Choice 3** Watch two short newscasts on graffiti artists. If freedom is "the right to do what you want," should graffiti artists have the right to create their art anywhere, even on someone else's property, without it being against the law? Write a persuasive paper to justify your point of view.
Choice 4 Freedom to appropriate art images. Take a look at the images in folder #7. Artists often get ideas from other artists' work. How would you feel if someone took your ideas and used them in their work? What if they took your work and made fun of it by changing it into something different than you intended? Justify your answers in your journal.	**Choice 5** Read the "Rockefeller Controversy" and debate the following issues of freedom: Did Diego Rivera, the artist of the mural, *Man at the Crossroads*, have the right to refuse to repaint the face, as requested by Mr. Rockefeller? Did Mr. Rockefeller have the right to destroy the mural? Justify your answers in your journal.	**Choice 6** *The Problem We All Live With,* 1964 Read about the topic of this artwork by Norman Rockwell. Does our freedom give us the right to treat other people any way we want? Does it give us the freedom to say and do whatever we want, even if it hurts others? Justify your answers in your journal.
Choice 7 Create a three-dimensional work that displays your consideration of the benefits of freedom and the costs.	**Choice 8** What does freedom mean to you? Create a podcast that expresses your ideas. Be sure to add in a minimum on ten images and a clear expression of your ideas. You may use narrative voice-over, other sound such as music, or rely on images alone.	**Choice 9** Read the article titled *Student Flag Project Draws Controversy* Consider the questions at the end of the article and answer them on the sheet and paste the article in your journal. Find one other person to discuss the issues of freedom that were brought up in this article.

Freedom Choice Board Contract

A.7.4

To demonstrate what I have explored and learned, I will complete the following three choices:
(Be sure that one of your choices is 1, 5, or 9, and another of your choices is 2, 7, or 8.)

Choice #____ **Choice #____** **Choice #____**

To help me stay on track and complete these choices by the deadline, I will:

If I fall behind or need help, I will do the following things to take responsibility for my work:

If I have extra time or complete my choices before the deadline, I will use my time wisely in the following ways:

Freedom is a choice I would like to have in this class, and I state that I am trustworthy enough to be given this responsibility.

Artist Name (Print): ________________________________

Artist Name (Signature): ________________________________ Date: ____/____/____

Art Mentor (Signature): ________________________________ Date: ____/____/____

Freedom: Choice 1

A.7.5

Norman Rockwell's paintings *Four Freedoms*

Name: ______________________ **Class:** ______________________

If you would have chosen the same four freedoms as Rockwell, describe why. If not, write about or sketch what four freedoms you believe *all* people should have. Please be sure to write in complete sentences and to justify all your answers with reasons to support your ideas.

Freedom: ______________________	**Freedom:** ______________________
Freedom: ______________________	**Freedom:** ______________________

Index